AUSTRALIAN NATIVES FOR YOUR GARDEN

Penelope A. Rose
John T. Rose
(Sydney Wildflower Nurseries)

Kangaroo Press

Acknowledgments

Anne Bird (Sydney Wildflower Nursery, North)
Phillip Congdon (Sydney Wildflower Nursery, South)
Mark Ferrington (Sydney Wildflower Nursery, West)
Photography: John T. Rose
Line Drawings: Pamela Polglase
Cover: Callistemon 'Little John'

This edition first published in 1984 by Kangaroo Press
3 Whitehall Road (P.O. Box 75) Kenthurst 2154
Typeset by G.T. Setters Pty Limited
Printed in Hong Kong by Colorcraft Ltd

ISBN 0 949924 86 5

Contents

Introduction	5
About Plants	8
Planning and Preparing for a Native Garden	10
Alphabetical List and Descriptions	15
Colour Plates	33
Orchids	68
Ferns	69
Plant Lists	71
Further Reading	77
List of Common Names	78

Passiflora
aurantia
Pam

Introduction

Australia's wildflowers are the result of many million years of separate development, and because of the particular conditions of climate and soil on this continent our native flora is very different from that found in any other part of the world. Unfortunately Australian gardeners have tended to use mainly imported species as garden subjects and our own beautiful and rare flora has been neglected. Only now when preservation of the flora is threatened by the continuing urban sprawl are gardeners starting to use and appreciate native plants around their home.

The desire for conservation can be combined with a visually satisfying minimum-maintenance garden but a basic understanding of the plants and their different requirements is essential.

In this book we introduce the reader to plants and their relationships and then discuss briefly the different aspects of planning and preparing for a native garden.

In gardening with native plants, however, there are no hard and fast rules. No two successful gardeners subscribe to the same philosophy, nor is there any reference to which one can turn and find the answer. Research into cultivation of native plants is still in its infancy, and natural habitat does not necessarily indicate a plant's requirements under cultivation.

Many different species are being brought into cultivation each year and it is not possible to list them all, but a broad range of plants suitable for the garden is generally found in most retail plant nurseries. Of course some of these will be only seasonally available, but the specialist native nurseries should be able to help year-round.

It is hoped that a love of native plants in the garden will grow to a love of native plants in the wild, and that readers will search and learn more about them. In National Parks where these plants are protected in their natural environment, the various plant associations can be seen and some understanding gained of the animals which depend upon them for survival.

This book is dedicated to the two organisations most closely associated with our aims:

THE SOCIETY FOR GROWING AUSTRALIAN PLANTS
and
THE NATIONAL PARKS & WILDLIFE SERVICE OF NSW

The Society for Growing Australian Plants (SGAP)

Whatever your interest in native plants, your task will prove a lot easier if you share your problems and successes with other people. Membership of this Society provides a forum for exchange of experiences and ideas. It was formed with the intention of encouraging and helping people to grow the plants which are native to this continent.

The Society publishes definitive works on the flora and the journal *Australian Plants* gives authoritative information on aspects of native plants and their cultivation which cannot be found elsewhere.

The Society for Growing Australian Plants is Australia-wide with self-contained Regional Councils in each state and in the ACT. There are eighteen local groups in New South Wales and contact is maintained with individuals in country areas where no group has been formed. Any member of the NSW Region of the Society is entitled to belong to any of the local groups.

Membership of a Region is on a subscription basis and members receive copies of the quarterly journal *Australian Plants* and a Region Newsletter. In addition, seeds of many Australian plants are available free. Regions and local groups all hold regular meetings and sponsor many other related activities, including exhibitions which demonstrate the beauty and range of Australian wildflowers.

Membership enquiries may be directed to any of the specialist native nurseries.

The National Parks & Wildlife Service of New South Wales (NPWS)

The NPWS is responsible for the conservation of representative samples of the NSW natural landscape and wildlife habitat. The environments of NSW are very varied, embracing arid western plains, rain-drenched north coast, cold alpine areas and wind-swept coastal dunes. Each of these provides peculiar conditions to which the indigenous wildlife is adapted, so the flower and plant communities of the state are diverse.

The Service protects such samples of woodland, heath, swamp or rainforest by the acquisition of unspoiled land. Dependent upon the management strategy used, such land is dedicated either as a National Park or Nature Reserve. Nature Reserves generally involve extremely small areas and as such are vulnerable to destruction by human use. Access to them is restricted.

National Parks are spacious areas of natural beauty set aside for the outstanding features of landscape as well as for the protection of the associated flora and fauna. Facilities and access routes are developed for public use in a way which will not unduly destroy the quality of wildness.

Recreational activities which cause a minimum of intrusion into the area are encouraged. These include photography, walking, climbing, camping, swimming, sailing, canoeing, studying and just relaxing. Walking trails, signs and interpretative facilities, and low-key camping areas are provided.

Because of the limited amount of land which the NPWS can acquire, the conservation of plant and animal species is augmented by the Service's Wildlife Refuge System in which areas of private property are managed for their wildlife values. The Service offers advice to land managers on the propagation and regeneration of native plants with an emphasis on the conservation of those trees and shrubs which are endemic to the area. Assistance is given with propagation from local seed stock and with the selection of other suitable species.

In the urban or metropolitan scene, landscaping with native plants is encouraged to entice native birds, reptiles and small mammals back into gardens where they can be enjoyed and observed around the home.

The Service publishes the magazine *Parks & Wildlife*, education monographs and literature on all aspects of its activities. Further information is available from District Offices throughout the state or from the Director, NPWS, P.O. Box N 189, Grosvenor Street PO, Sydney.

Other Places to Visit — Sydney

Bankstown Council Wildflower Garden,
7 Sylvan Grove, Picnic Point
Open 9 am–3 pm weekdays. Weekends (mid-August to November only) 9 am–5 pm. An area of approximately 1 ha. set in natural bushland has been planted with Australian native species from all over the continent. Included is an excellent display of Kangaroo Paw (*Anigozanthos*) and a natural moist gully in which are found many superb ferns and native orchids.

Joseph Banks Native Plant Garden,
Bates Drive, Kareela
Open 10 am–3 pm daily. An area of approximately 2 ha. of display gardens including waterfalls and ponds. A testing area for new species. A very large range of unusual and endangered species. Barbecue facilities are available. It is run by Sutherland Council and supported by the Sutherland SGAP.

Katandra Bushland Sanctuary,
Lane Cove Road, Ingleside
Open every Sunday August through October, every third Sunday rest of year. This sanctuary contains only indigenous plants and is preserved in its native state with paths running through its several plant communities, open forest, sclerophyll forest and rain forest. A large number of interesting trees and understorey plants including *Boronia* species are preserved. Managed by a Trust appointed by the Lands Department, it is supported by a Bushland Club.

Ku-ring-gai Wildflower Garden,
Mona Vale Road, St Ives
Open every day (except Good Friday, Christmas Day) 10 am–4 pm. This is a huge garden of some 130 ha. with 6–7 km of walking trails mainly through natural bushland but with a number of introduced trees and shrubs, mostly labelled. There is an excellent shade house with ferns and orchids from rainforest areas. Kiosk open at weekends. Managed by the Ku-ring-gai Municipal Council.

Stony Range Flora Reserve,
Pittwater Road, Dee Why
Open every day except Public Holidays, 10 am–4 pm. This reserve of just over 3 ha. is managed for Warringah Shire Council (as trustees for the Lands Department) by a voluntary committee. It is mostly typical Hawkesbury sandstone flora but a wide variety of native species from different parts of Australia have been added. The garden has an extensive system of pathways crossing it to enable the visitor to fully appreciate its different characteristics.

Other Places to Visit — NSW Country

Burrendong Arboretum,
near Burrendong Dam, Wellington, NSW
Easily accessible by bitumen road, the turnoff plainly marked from either the Molong–Wellington or Stuart Town–Wellington roads, the Arboretum is a splendid display of more than 1600 species. With over 30 000 plants including huge collections of *Eucalyptus*, *Acacia*, *Melaleuca*, *Hakea*, *Grevillea*, *Callistemon* and *Prostanthera* species, late winter and early spring provide the best flowering display. The Arboretum is supported by voluntary subscription. Information regarding membership of the Arboretum Association can be obtained from the Treasurer, "Moonee-Nyrang", Wellington, 2820.

Canberra Botanic Gardens,
Clunies Ross Street, Canberra
The Botanic Gardens at Canberra comprise 40 ha. devoted entirely to native flora, primarily for research and experimentation but open to the public for their inspection and information. All plants are labelled and informative brochures are available. A large area of simulated rainforest is of particular interest.

Wirrimbirra Sanctuary, Hume Highway, Bargo
This is a National Trust property under the control of the David G. Stead Memorial Wildlife Foundation. It embraces an area of almost 100 ha. of bushland sanctuary, part of which has been established as a Wildflower Garden with Study Nature Trails and name-plated plants. Facilities and accommodation for students at all levels are provided. The Foundation publishes a quarterly News Sheet and a series of other educational booklets in the *Your Australian Garden* series. The Nursery propagates and sells a range of native plants. Membership and other enquiries to Box 4840, GPO, Sydney.

About Plants

Naming Plants

Australian wildflowers have few popular names and many of these are local in origin. Christmas Bush, for example, refers to *Ceratopetalum gummiferum* in NSW, *Prostanthera lasianthos* in Victoria and *Nuytsia floribunda* in WA.

As with most nurseries, botanic nomenclature is used throughout this text. Some popular names are noted and a list of those most commonly in use is given in the Appendix. No guarantee is given, however, that the authors' interpretation will necessarily lead to the expected plant.

Many different forms of leaf type and plant growth (tree, climber, etc.) are found within a range of plants which are in actual fact very closely related through their flower and fruit structure. Such plants form a **Genus** (as *Eucalyptus*). Within each genus are a number of **species**. Plants of a particular species have constant and distinctive features, although some variation may occur in flower colour or leaf shape. As examples, *Callistemon citrinus* may be found with white or red flowers, *Myoporum parvifolium* with at least four different leaf forms.

A group of **Genera** with related features (such as *Callistemon, Calothamnus, Leptospermum, Eucalyptus*) are grouped together into the broader classification of **Family** (*Myrtaceae*).

Types of Plants

A very simplified division of the plant kingdom is given here.

The plants which we cultivate (ferns, conifers, flowering plants) are *vascular* plants, that is, they have stems, roots and leaves and a specialised internal system for conducting water and nutrients throughout the plant.

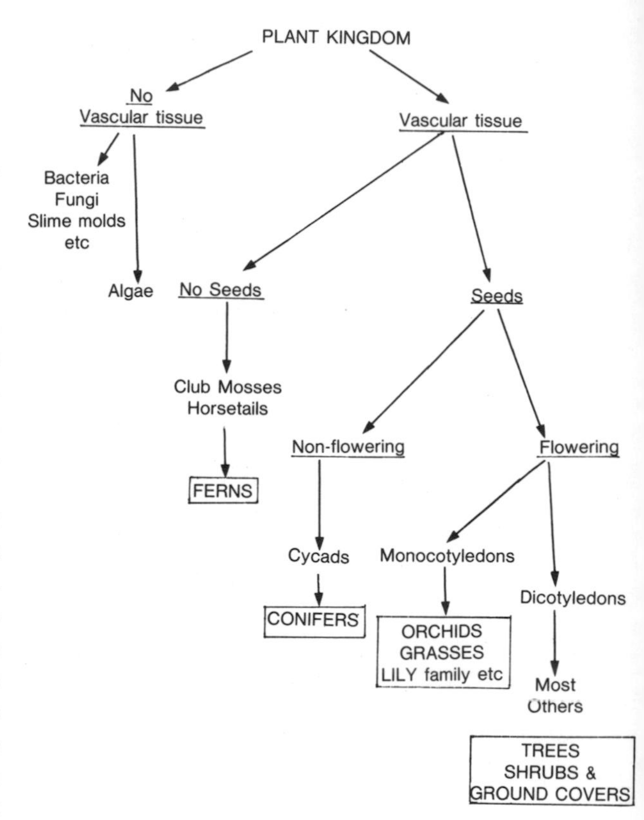

Ferns

The ferns most obviously differ from the 'higher' forms of life in their method of reproduction. The fern life cycle comprises three stages: *spore*, *prothallus* and *fern plant* itself. The spores appear as 'dust' on the backs of the fern leaves or *fronds*. Each spore grows into a tiny kidney-shaped body, the prothallus, and it is this that carries out a function similar to a flower and represents the sexual phase of the fern's life cycle. Only after fertilisation will the first tiny frond of the fern plant unfurl.

Propagation of ferns may be by division in creeping species, from bulbils in others or from spore development. On a commercial scale they are also produced by tissue culture.

Conifers

These plants are non-flowering but reproduce their kind from seed and include species such as *Araucaria*, *Podocarpus* and *Callitris*. They are all cone-bearing and the seeds are not enclosed within a fruit of any kind.

Flowering Plants

By far the majority of plants bought for the home garden are flowering types. The flower is the climax to the plant's existence and contains the parts necessary for reproduction. The *calyx* comprises the *sepals* which protect the flower in bud and the *corolla* is formed from the colourful *petals*. The reproductive parts within the *corolla* comprise a number of *stamens* (long *filaments* bearing the pollen-containing *anthers*) and a stalk-like *style* with its swollen end, the *stigma*. The *stigma* receives the pollen brought by a pollinating agent (bird, wind, insect, etc.) from another flower on the same or different plant.

At the base of the stigma is the *ovary*. The *fruit* containing the *seed* is formed from this ovary after fertilisation. Fruits take on many different forms, all related to the method of seed dispersal, for example nuts, fleshy berries, etc.

In the Australian flora many interesting adaptations from the standard flower structure have resulted in a wealth of varied and unusual flower arrangements.

The Flowering Plants fall into two divisions, *monocotyledons* which have one 'seed' leaf and *dicotyledons* which have two 'seed' leaves upon germination.

Monocotyledonous plants characteristically have flower parts mostly arranged in threes and their leaves are parallel-veined. Species such as *Patersonia*, *Anigozanthos* and *Doryanthes* are typical. They also include the unusual Orchid family. Propagation is by seed or division.

By far the largest number of garden plants are dicotyledons. In these plants the flower parts are generally in fours or fives. They range from huge trees to ground cover and mat plants. Propagation is generally from seed or cutting, although the latter is probably preferable as it allows for the production of plants selected for good form and flower.

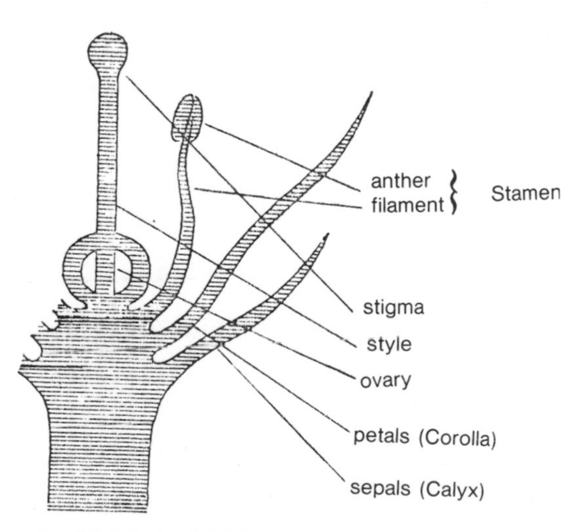

DIAGRAMMATIC SECTION OF FLOWER

Planning and Preparing for a Native Garden

Site Preparation

Some native plants will prosper without any garden preparation but to attempt to grow them all like this must produce failures.

Good drainage is essential for the survival of many native plant species. If the garden is not already well drained then this must be given first consideration. On a level site adequate drainage may be quite simply achieved by raising the level of garden beds by approximately 30 cm using timber logs, bush rock, brick or similar retaining materials. Care must be taken not to build soil around the base of existing trees since this may cause collar rot and eventual death. Where garden beds cannot be raised it may be necessary to effect satisfactory drainage with the use of agricultural pipes.

Most native plants seem to prefer acid soils. In fact the majority of species originating on the east coast of Australia show adverse reaction to soil alkalinity. However, a tolerance of neutral and more alkaline conditions appears to increase westwards across the continent, with some Western species showing a preference for this condition.

It is not true that all Australian native plants prefer light sandy soils; even those naturally occurring on poor soils prefer something rather richer. Where the soil is very poor it is wise to dig in some organic material such as peat moss, compost or animal manure before planting or the plants may tend to grow tall and straggly.

A large range of native plants will, however, readily adapt to growing in either light, medium or heavy soil conditions. Heavy soils, while unlikely to maintain species from areas such as the Hawkesbury sandstone, are often better suited to species such as the inland *Eremophilas*, some *Prostantheras* and even members of the East Coast Pea family such as *Indigofera australis*. Generally speaking, the heavier the soil type the more compact the growth form and the closer together the specimens grow without undue evidence of competition.

Clay subsoils exposed as a result of deep excavation work are extremely unsuitable; even the hardy *Melaleucas* will object. Where this is the case it is wise to import new weed-free topsoil to build up the garden beds.

Choice of Plants

Because the Australian continent embraces such a wide range of climate, soil type and exposure, some suitable species can be selected for almost any situation. There is also no reason why they cannot be grown in close association with many exotic plants.

Consider first the local climate. Should this influence your choice of plants? Are you in a coastal or inland position? Is there a high or low rainfall? Do you experience frost conditions?

Those who live in areas subject to mild or severe frosts are wise to plant initially species known to tolerate these conditions. After the garden is established and some protection can be provided, then it is the time to experiment with the less frost-tolerant plants. It is probably wise to plant these at a larger size at the beginning of spring to allow for a full growth period and stimulate stem thickening before the winter cold sets in.

Only a minority of plants occur naturally in coastline conditions and some of these can be used to provide a screen from salt spray and thus present less tolerant species with protection. Remember that immediately after a severe storm some salt can be washed from leaf surfaces with a hand-held hose.

Care should be taken that plants for exposed conditions are not too soft. Plants grown under shade or pushed with liquid fertiliser under conditions of warmth and humidity are ill-equipped to withstand extremes of temperature, strong or salt-laden winds.

Having decided the restrictions which your locality is likely to place on your choice of plants, plan next the provision of background or screening for the garden.

In the text we have tried to distinguish between trees and shrubs on the basis of shape rather than size. A plant is designated *shrub* where bushiness extends to the ground and as *tree* where a definite trunk supporting a head of foliage is its normal form.

Never go for an 'instant' effect by purchasing the largest plants available. A plant which is too large for its pot is unlikely to do well in the ground. Rather purchase a small plant in a large pot.

In selection of smaller growing and ground cover species special attention must be given to height and spread and care taken that larger species are not planted so that they block out the smaller ones. Many ground cover species require plenty of sun and will probably make unsatisfactory growth if planted under tall trees where there is too much shade and the added problem of competition for water. Fern species are often more suitable for under-storey planting.

It is also sensible to include a few leguminous (pea-flowering) plants. These species through their association with bacteria in the soil are able to enrich the soil in which they are planted. The pea family, Fabaceae, is very diverse, ranging from tree species to groundcovers.

The final consideration before plant selection is flowering time. In the Coastal and Dividing Ranges of NSW there is a fairly regular pattern of rainfall and flowering times are predictable, although they may vary slightly from garden to garden. Further inland, where rainfall is low, flowering is often prompted by good falls of rain and less easy to predict.

Some genera, such as *Acacia*, provide a flowering species for each month of the year. August to October, being spring, sees the largest number of native plants in bloom. Gardens rapidly change colour as the yellows of early-flowering *Acacia* species give way to the pinks of the *Boronias*, then the blues of the *Prostantheras* and finally the reds and pinks of *Callistemons*. A continuity of flowering through summer to winter months, however, will require more careful planning.

Planting

Before planting arrange selected plants in position, giving particular consideration to height and spread. It is difficult to control the size of larger growing plants and care should be taken with the smaller species to provide them with plenty of room.

1. Soak the plant thoroughly before removing it from the container. This can be done by standing it in a bucket of water while you prepare the hole. You can even add some liquid fertiliser and root stimulant.

2. Dig the hole at least twice the width of the plant container and about the same depth, making sure to break up thoroughly all the soil at the bottom of the hole.

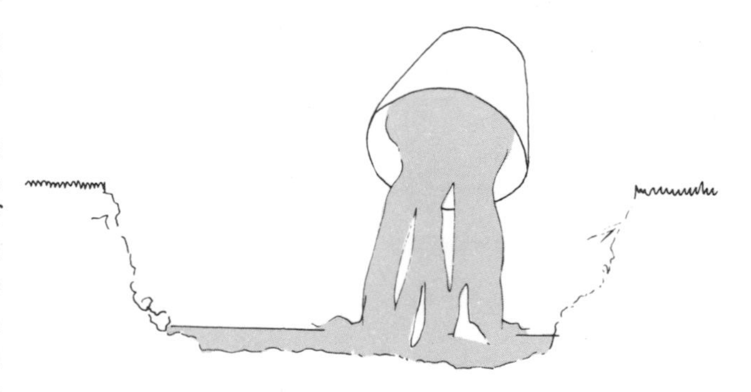

3. Fill hole with water and allow it to drain away. If soil is very dry, repeat a second time.

4. Add slow release fertiliser, about a tablespoonful, and thoroughly mix with the soil at the bottom of the hole.

5. Remove plant carefully from container by placing hand so second and third fingers surround the trunk or stem and support the soil mass. Tap container gently against brick or similar edge to release.

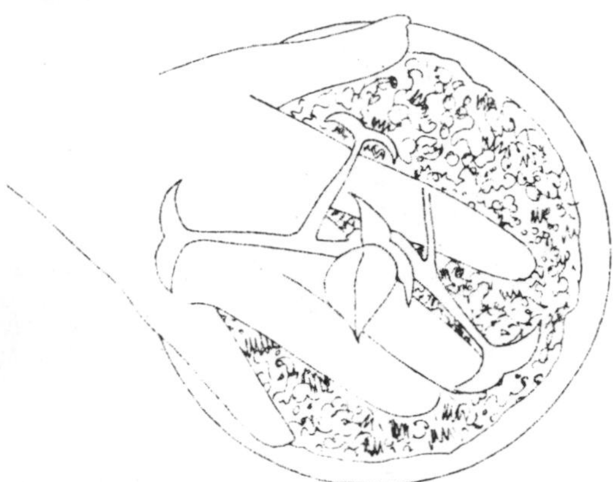

6. Inspect root system, taking care not to break the main root or disturb major root branches. Carefully remove old brown dense matted roots and any damaged roots, using sharp secateurs. Roots should not be coiled at the bottom of the container in normal healthy plants. There are one or two extremely dense root-forming plants (e.g. *Westringia*) where this does happen in even very young container grown plants.

7. Place plant in hole carefully, ensuring soil level is slightly below the garden soil level. Staking is not necessary for young plants as they usually grow stronger without them.

8. Backfill hole with soil and take care to press it down firmly around the soil bole of the plant so it is firmly in place.

9. Water well with at least a couple of buckets full of water or repeated waterings with lesser amount if penetration is difficult to obtain.

10. Mulch if desired, taking care not to take mulch right up to trunk or stem of plant.

Note: For planting in *shallow soils* where the topsoil butts immediately onto heavy sticky clay beneath (often the case with a new home for which excavation is done), build up soil to such a height that the plant's roots will be just above the subsoil and the diameter of the mound is at least 1 metre to prevent drying out.

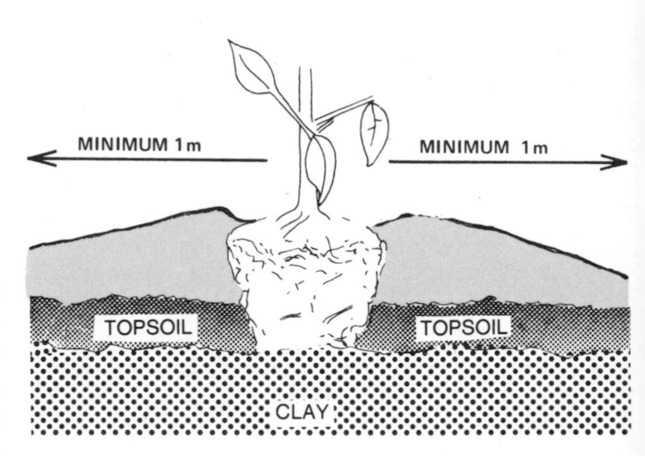

Do not neglect your plants in the first few weeks after planting. Remember that in the nursery situation they have been watered at least daily. It should be sufficient to give the plants a thorough soaking about once a fortnight or, in hot weather, once a week until they are established.

If it is necessary to keep plants in their containers after purchase for any time, take particular care with their watering. When watering with a hand-held hose the surface may look wet and water appear to be pouring out at the bottom of the pot while the soil in the pot is still quite dry. It may be more satisfactory to water such container plants every day with a fixed sprinkler over a period of, say, half an hour.

Many native plants have feeder roots near the surface which should be kept cool and not disturbed. This is the reason why transplanting plants from bushland, apart from being illegal, is seldom successful and this is the same for plants in the garden once they are established.

A layer of mulch will help keep feeder roots cool and also retain moisture in the garden. If spread thickly enough it may also help to keep down the weeds. If available, an ideal mulch is natural garden debris such as leaves and branches which can be broken up and thrown onto the garden. Pine bark and wood chip mulch which have been left to weather also provide a satisfactory cover. Some native plant gardeners prefer to use an inert material such as coarse sand or gravel, but whatever the mulch used it is wiser to keep it away from the stems of the plants themselves to prevent stem rot.

Garden Care and Maintenance

Your native garden provides you with relatively low maintenance. However all plants benefit from regular *light* applications of fertiliser to keep them lush. It is also wise to tip prune regularly during the growing season. This should be done from a very small size to ensure a bushier and more attractive specimen. Flowers and straggly growth should also be removed after flowering before the plant wastes energy producing seed. This may often produce another flowering. Take care not to prune into old wood. A few plants resent pruning and if you are unsure give only a very light pruning at first.

Some plants may also need staking to prevent wind damage. Your nursery proprietor is the best person to advise on this as in some species staking may prevent the formation of a strong tap root and self-supporting stem.

Naturally there will be birds in your native garden which feed on the honey, seeds and fruits, and help to control the attendant pests. If you can, pick off any pests and destroy them. If this is not possible, identify them and then attack with the appropriate low-toxicity pesticide, *used exactly as recommended.* Remember not to spray on a windy day and take care to keep the container away from children.

Scale infestations are caused by insects and are most commonly found on *Eucalyptus* and *Melaleuca* species and members of the family Rutaceae. They may appear as a white or brown crusty covering on the stems and at the early stage can be rubbed off, or a whole branch can be removed and burned. If the infestation is heavy it should be treated with White Oil.

Fungi are the cause of rusts and downy mildews and these can be wiped off with cotton wool and methylated spirits at an early stage. However they can spread very rapidly, especially in humid conditions, and a commercially available fungicide may have to be applied.

Leaf-chewing insects may be controlled with contact insecticides but first make sure the damage is not being caused by nocturnal slugs or snails.

Web-building insects tend to attack *Leptospermum* species and if the web cannot be removed by hand it will be necessary to spray with an insecticide before the bush is defoliated and dies.

Galls are often found disfiguring the leaves of *Eucalypt* species. They are not usually killers and the parrot family will help in their control. In a young tree galls can be cut off and burned and growth stimulated with an appropriate fertiliser.

Borers are the chief enemy of *Acacia* and *Banksia* species and usually give themselves away with a crumbly exudate from their hole. The boring insect should be dug out immediately with a flexible piece of wire. Methylated spirits or insecticide can be poured into the hole before it is sealed with soap or similar sealant.

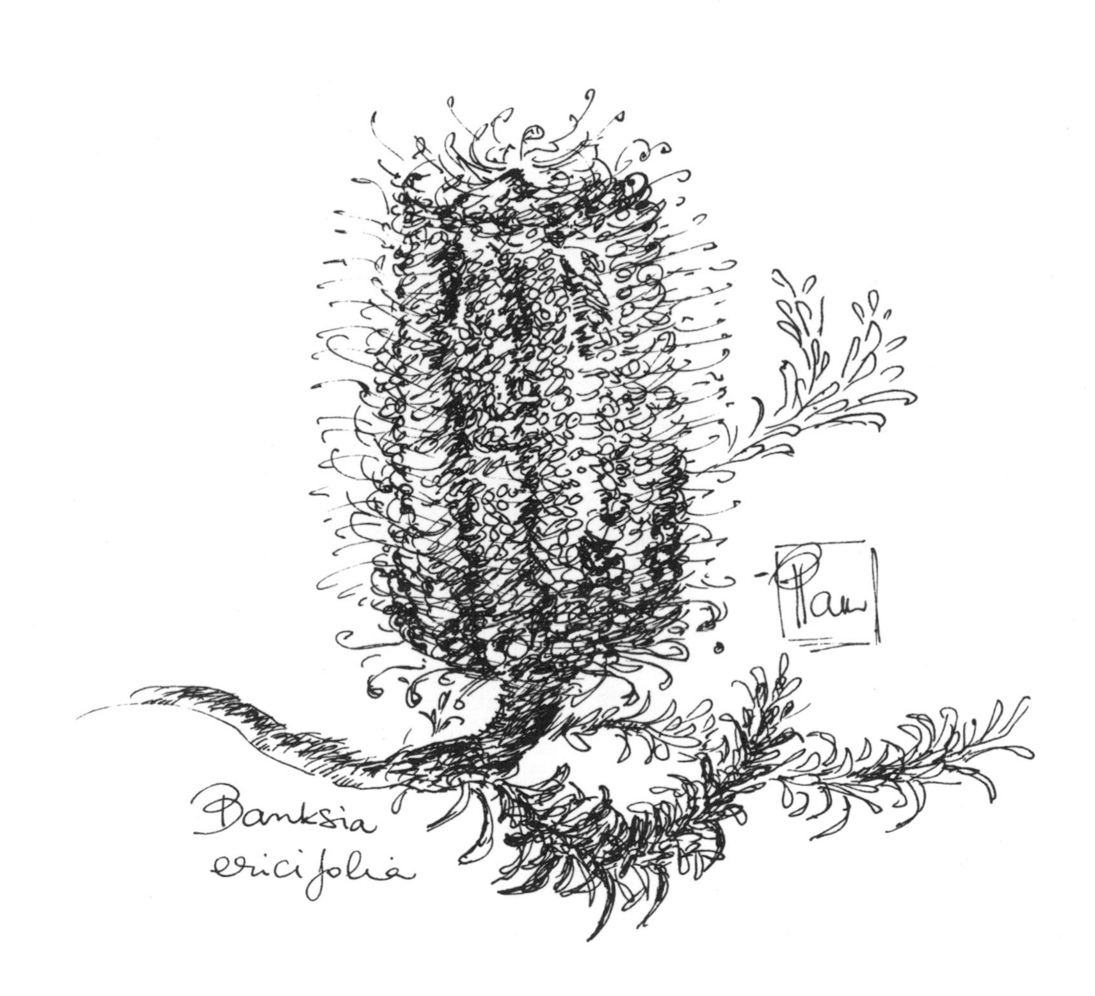
Banksia
ericifolia

Alphabetical List and Descriptions

Plants found naturally in NSW are so indicated (N). For other plants, the *nearest* state only is indicated.

The heights given are those to which the plant is expected to grow in *average home garden* conditions. They should be regarded more as a guide than absolute.

Unless otherwise indicated, plants will all tolerate normal sunny positions.

ACACIA (Wattle)
Family: Fabaceae

All Acacia seedlings produce a feathery bipinnate leaf, but in many species this is replaced in the adult plant by a flattened leaf stalk (phyllode). Phyllode shape and size is characteristic for a species.

Individual flowers are minute and their colours range from pale cream to brilliant golds. Flowers are arranged in groups of as few as 10 to as many as 70, shaped as balls or rods, giving the whole flowerhead a fluffy appearance. Flowering time may vary slightly from year to year, but usually lasts about six weeks. By careful selection it is possible to have a wattle in bloom for every month of the year.

Although the majority are quick growers, many have only a relatively short life (say 8–15 years). They may all be kept bushy with gentle pruning, especially after flowering.

adunca 5 × 4 m
(Wallangarra Wattle). Upright, shapely, slow-growing tree with narrow phyllodes, but retaining its juvenile foliage quite late. Magnificent scented gold balls in winter. Well-drained spot. (N) **Plate 1**

armata 2 × 2 m
(Kangaroo Thorn). Fast growing, hardy shrub with small wavy phyllodes and spines. Gold balls in spring. Very hardy. (N)

baileyana 6 × 5 m
(Cootamundra Wattle). Large bushy shrub, fine grey feathery leaves, deep yellow balls in winter. Frost and drought resistant. (N). Also purple-leaved form. (N) **Plate 2**

beckleri 1–3 m × 2 m
(Barrier Range Wattle). Erect or spreading shrub with blue-green foliage, red and shining when young. Bright yellow ball flowers late winter to spring. (N) **Plate 3**

boormanni 5 × 4 m
(Snowy River Wattle). Bushy shrub with narrow dark-green phyllodes and deep gold balls in spring. Frost resistant. (N) ***Plate 4***

brownii 1 m
(Prickly Moses). Low shrub with spiny phyllodes and large golden balls in winter. Frost resistant. (N)

buxifolia 2–4 m
(Box-leaved Wattle). Handsome shrub or small tree with spectacular dense heads of golden ball flowers spring and summer. Very hardy. Frost resistant (N)

cardiophylla 3 × 2 m
(Wyalong Wattle). Tiny light-green feathery foliage and brilliant yellow balls late winter. For sunny, dry position. (N) **Plate 5**

cognata 4–6 m × 6 m
Open rounded shrub of drooping habit, cream flowers in spring. (N)

conferta 3 × 2 m
(Golden Top). Small narrow grey-green phyllodes pressed against stems. Solitary golden balls at branch ends from autumn to winter. For heavy soils, open position. (N)

cultriformis 3 × 3 m
(Knife-leaf Wattle). Arching habit. Grey-green triangular phyllodes and masses of gold balls in spring. (N) **Plate 6**

dealbata 6–10 m
(Silver Wattle). Erect, small tree with smooth silver-mottled trunk and bipinnate leaves. Yellow ball flowers late winter to spring. Prefers moist soils. (N)

deanii 4 m
Shapely small tree with bipinnate foliage. Pale lemon balls most of year. Adaptable. (N)

decora 1.5 × 1 m
(Showy Wattle). Bushy, graceful shrub with pale narrow phyllodes and long sprays of gold flowers late winter to spring. Suitable for hedging in hot, dry position. Frost resistant. (N) **Plate 7**

decurrens 12 m
(Early Black Wattle). Dark-green feathery fine leaves and

brilliant yellow flowers late winter. For any position. Quick growing. Frost resistant. (N) **Plate 8**

drummondii 1.5 × 1 m
(Drummond's Wattle). Small bushy shrub with pinnate leaves and yellow spikes early spring. Sheltered, well-drained position. (W)

elata 12 m
(Cedar Wattle). Tall, graceful tree with large bipinnate leaves, bronze-tipped when young. Creamy balls in summer. For moist soils. (N)

elongata 2.5 m
(Swamp Wattle). Long slender shrub with fine graceful phyllodes and clusters of single-ball flowers in spring. Short-lived, but adaptable and fast-growing. (N)

fimbriata 6 m
(Fringed Wattle). Bushy shrub or small tree with small lanceolate phyllodes. Numerous sprays of brilliant, yellow flowers late winter. Frost resistant. (N) **Plate 9**

floribunda 4 m
(White Sally). Small to medium spreading tree with somewhat pendulous habit, long narrow phyllodes. Pale-yellow, scented, but enormous florescence. Heavy soils (N)

glaucescens 10 m
(Coast Myall). Beautiful small tree with silvery-grey curved phyllodes and long yellow fingers in late spring. Suitable for coast. (N) **Plate 10**

gracilifolia 2.5 m
Medium-sized, bushy shrub with very fine long foliage and deep-yellow spike florescence. Excellent garden subject, hardy and adaptable, attractive even when not in flower. (SA)

howittii 4–5 cm
(Sticky Acacia). Small weeping tree with small, sticky, closely packed phyllodes. Masses of pale-cream scented flowers in spring. Adaptable and very fast growing. (V) **Plate 11**

iteaphylla 3 × 2 m
(Gawler Range Wattle). Attractive spreading shrub with long, narrow, fine phyllodes, mauve-tipped when young. Beautiful clear light-yellow flowers in winter. (SA) **Plate 12**

jibberdingensis 3 m
Slender bright-green phyllodes, hooked at ends, drooping habit. Beautiful golden spike flowers in early winter and often after rain. Adaptable for well-drained position. (W)

linearifolia 6 m
(Stringybark Wattle). Magnificent shapely tree. Long, narrow, slightly glaucous phyllodes and gold flowers in early spring. For any conditions. (N)

lineata 2 m
Bushy shrub with short, narrow, dark-green phyllodes closely packed on branches. Brilliant inflorescence of small deep yellow ball flowers right up stem, early spring. Easy. (N)

linifolia 3 m
(Flax Wattle). Tall, slender, graceful shrub with narrow dark-green phyllodes and beautiful florescence of creamy flower sprays in summer and at other times. Easy. (N)

longifolia 4 m
(Sydney Golden Wattle). Upright bushy shrub with long phyllodes and golden-rod flowers late winter. Adaptable. Frost resistant. (N)
var. *sophorae*
As above, but mostly prostrate in habit. Sand binder.

longissima 4 m
Graceful shrub with long, narrow phyllodes and cream flower spikes in summer. Prefers moist conditions. (N)

mearnsii 10 m
Fast-growing tree with fine bipinnate leaves and pale yellow flowers in terminal heads late spring. Frost resistant. (V)

melanoxylon to 30 m
(Blackwood). Tall upright tree with dense crown of dark green leathery foliage. Extremely hardy and fast growing. (N)

parramattensis 10 m
Fast growing tree with fine bipinnate foliage. Cream ball flowers in summer. (N)

podalyriifolia 4 × 4 m
(Queensland Silver Wattle). Broad, oval, silvery-grey phyllodes and gold ball flowers in early winter. Fast growing. Hardy. (Q) **Plate 13**

pravissima 4–5 m
(Oven's Wattle). Attractive olive-green triangular weeping foliage and yellow balls in spring. Sunny, moist position. Frost resistant. (N)

prominens 7 m
(Gosford Wattle). Neat, compact tree with rounded phyllodes, slightly weeping habit and yellow flower balls in spring. Frost resistant. (N)

pulchella 1 × 2 m
(Prickly Moses). Leaves fine with spine at base. Gold-yellow balls in abundance. Good spreading rockery shrub, short-lived but self-seeding. Hardy. (W)

pycnantha 4–5 × 3 m
(Golden Wattle, Australia's national floral emblem). Broad, curved phyllodes, often leathery. Deep golden balls in spring. Suitable for dry, shallow, exposed positions. (N)

rotundifolia 2 × 2 m
(Round-leaf Wattle). Attractive shrub with rounded phyllodes and golden ball flowers in spring. For well-drained semi-shade positions. (N)

saligna 5–7 m
(Golden Wreath). Rounded shrub with pendulous foliage and large golden balls late winter. Tolerates wet, heavy soils. Suitable for coast. (W) **Plate 14**

spectabilis 4 m
(Mudgee Wattle). Grey-green leaves and showy rich yellow balls in long sprays. Frost and drought resistant. (N)

suaveolens 1.5 m
(Sweet Scented Wattle). Dense shrub with largish single-veined phyllodes. Cylindrical spikes in winter. For open, well-drained position. Frost resistant. (N)

subulata 3 m
Slender, graceful small shrub with light green phyllodes and pale flowerheads for most of year. (N)

terminalis 2 m
(Sunshine Wattle). Shiny dark green bipinnate foliage, bronze when young. Yellow flowerheads late summer to early winter. For sheltered, moist positions. (N)

vestita 4 m
(Weeping Boree). Dense shrub, weeping habit, small greyish phyllodes and hairy branches. Brilliant yellow flower balls late winter to spring. For dry positions. Frost resistant. Prune hard after flowering. (N)

ACMENA (Lilly-Pilly) Family: Myrtaceae

smithii 10 m
(Lilly-Pilly). Bushy upright tree with shiny leaves often bronze at tips. Masses of cream fluffy flowers in winter. Edible violet berries. Can be trimmed. (N)

ACTINOTUS Family: Apiaceae

helianthi 30 cm
(Flannel Flower). Compound greyish-white woolly leaves and cream daisy-like flowers. Biennial, but self-seeding. Requires sandy soil. (Syd) **Plate 15**

AGONIS Family: Myrtaceae

flexuosa 5–7 × 5 m
(Weeping Myrtle). Graceful drooping foliage, rusty at tips. Rugged bark. Small white flowers along stems in spring. Suitable for mild coastal conditions. Variegated form sometimes available. (W)

***flexuosa* 'Nana'** 2 m × 1.5 m
Attractive, dwarf shrub suitable for pot culture and rockeries. (W)

linearifolia 3 m × 2 m
Upright, bushy shrub with fine hardy foliage and greyish-white flower clusters during spring and summer. Hardy. (W)

juniperina 4.5 m × 2 m
(Native Cedar). Excellent small bushy tree with fine clustered leaves and masses of small white flowers late spring to summer. For well-drained position. (W)

ALBIZIA Family: Mimosaceae

lophantha 4–6 m
(Cape Wattle). Bushy, fast-growing tree with bipinnate leaves and dense spikes of greenish-yellow flowers. Suitable for poor and dry conditions. Salt tolerant. (Syd)

ALYOGYNE Family: Malvaceae

huegelii 2 m
(Lilac Hibiscus). Lovely shrub with divided soft mid-green foliage and large open lilac flowers, some with red centres, in summer. Suited to hot, well-drained position. Cut back hard after flowering. (W) **Plate 16**

ANGOPHORA (Apple Myrtle) Family: Myrtaceae

Large and small trees, very similar to *Eucalypts*. Leaves are opposite and flower bud has no cap, flowers have petals.

bakeri 4–5 m × 4 m
(Narrow-leaved Apple). Small tree with straight trunk and narrow lanceolate leaves. Comparatively large. White flowers in summer. (Syd)

costata 12 m × 10 m
(Sydney Red Gum). Smooth bark which takes on many hues, red-orange-purple. Cream flowers in summer. (Syd)

floribunda 20 m × 4.5 m
(Rough-barked Apple). Attractive reddish and green foliage, large cream flowers in summer. Tall growing, but thrives in poor, sandy soils. (Syd)

hispida 2.5 m × 4 m
(Dwarf Apple). Long red-tipped leaves with reddish hairs on young branches. Large cream flowers in summer. For sunny, well-drained position. (Syd) **Plate 17**

ANIGOZANTHOS (Kangaroo Paw) Family: Haemodoraceae

Found only in Western Australia, where *A. manglesii* is the state's floral emblem, this family consists of herbs with flat strap-shaped leaves, folded at the midrib, arising from short rhizomes. The unusual 'paw' flowers arise in spikes on top of long stems. May be separated in autumn. Excellent for pot plants. Bird attractors.

'Dwarf Delight' to 1 m
(*flavidus* × *onycis*). Superb cultivar with orange-yellow flowers in profusion for warmer months. Ideal rockery plant.

flavidus 2 m
(Tall Yellow Kangaroo Paw). Hardy species which forms a large bushy clump. Flowers small and yellow (or red) in clusters. Attractive to honey-eating birds. Frost resistant. **Plate 18**

flavidus* × *manglesii 1–1.5 m
Red and green flowers borne on reddish stems during spring and summer.

manglesii 50 cm
(Red-and-Green Kangaroo Paw). Pale blue-green leaves, which are subject to black discoloration known as 'ink disease'. Striking red-and-green flowers. Prefers warm, well-drained position, but unsuited to humid coastal conditions. **Plate 19**

pulcherrimus 2 m
Greyish-green leaves and brilliant gold flowers in early summer. Prefers drier climate. (W)

'Red Cross' 2m
(*rufus* × *flavidus*). Another superb hybrid with burgundy-red coloured flowers and olive-green foliage. Very hardy and long flowering.

'Regal Claw' 2 m
(*flavidus* × *preissii*). Olive-green foliage and masses of orange and red flowers for long periods in spring and summer. **Plate 20**

viridis 30 cm
(Green Kangaroo Paw). Striking emerald-green paws, deep green fine leaves. Adaptable, but prefers sandy soils, wet in winter.

ASTARTEA Family: Myrtaceae

fascicularis 1 m
Upright, open shrub with fine foliage and white flowers for many months. Very hardy and suitable for cut flowers. Frost resistant. (W)

heteranthera 30–50 cm
Slender, attractive shrub with short needle-like leaves. Sprays of white flowers cover bush in summer. Adaptable. (W)

AUSTROMYRTUS Family: Myrtaceae

dulcis 50 cm–1 m × 30 cm
(Midyim). Attractive spreading small bush with pink new growth. White flowers in summer, followed by edible white berries. For sandy soils. (Q)

tenuifolia 1–2 m × 1 m
Small-growing shrub, bearing small white flowers in summer–autumn, followed by fleshy berry. Suitable for damp, sheltered position. (N)

BACKHOUSIA Family: Myrtaceae

citriodora 6 m
(Lemon-scented Myrtle). Bushy shrub with lemon-scented foliage and conspicuous creamy flowers in spring. Suitable for sunny, moist conditions, protected from wind. Excellent host for epiphytic orchids. (Q)

BAECKEA Family: Myrtaceae

Comprising small trees and shrubs, all with a profusion of small tea-tree-like flowers from spring to early summer. All respond to regular light pruning.

astarteoides 50 cm × 1 m
Dainty small shrub with tiny leaves and pink flowers in summer. Suitable for both dry and moist conditions, hardy. (W)

crenatifolia 3 m × 2 m
(Fern-Leaf Baeckea). Attractive shrub with small leaves and white flowers. For moist, semi-shade positions. (N)

densifolia 1 m × 50 cm
Upright shrub with crowded narrow leaves and white flowers in spring. For sun or semi-shade. (N)

imbricata 1 m × 1 m
Extremely hardy shrub with tiny leaves and tiny white star flowers in spring and summer. Suitable for exposed coastal positions. (N)

linifolia 2 m × 2 m
(Weeping Baeckea). Fine shrub with weeping, often bronze-tipped foliage. Small white flowers autumn to summer. For sunny, light, moist soils, coast or inland. (N)

ramosissima 30 cm × 1–2 m
Small undershrub suitable for rockeries. Tiny pale pink flowers, mostly in summer, but also other times. For sunny, well-drained position. (N)

virgata 3 m × 2 m
(Twiggy Baeckea). Fine willowy foliage and small white flowers in summer. Appreciates summer watering. Prune lightly after flowering. Frost resistant. (N)

***virgata* 'Dwarf'** 30 cm × 50 cm
Hardy, small spreading, flat-topped shrub with masses of tiny white flowers in late spring. Easily grown. Prefers sunny moist position.

***virgata* 'Miniature'** 30 cm × 50 cm
Hardy small shrub with bronzed new growth and dense, dark green foliage. Excellent rockery shrub and very hardy. Suitable for sunny moist position.

BANKSIA Family: Proteaceae

Shrubs and trees with rough brownish-grey trunks and tough leaves. Flowers are arranged in dense spikes (cones or brushes), which turn woody and are often used for decoration. Individual flowers are similar to *Grevillea*, with either hooked or straight style. As many as 1000 flowers may be found on a single cone. Excellent for bird attraction.

aspleniifolia 2 m
Tall shrub with irregularly toothed leaves and round, pale yellow cones. For moist, poor soils. Frost resistant. (N)

collina 3 m
(*spinulosa* var. *collina*, Hill Banksia). Large stiff shrub with toothed narrow leaves, white below. Honey-coloured cones in winter. Easy to grow. Frost resistant. (N)

ericifolia 4 m × 3 m
(Heath Banksia). Dense bushy shrub or small tree with crowded small leaves. Flower cones autumn to winter, usually orange but red and yellows also found. Suited to any position, including coast. (N) **Plate 21**

'Giant Candles' 4 m × 3 m
(*spinulosa* × *ericifolia*). Tall, hardy shrub noted for huge brushes 30–40 cm long and orange in colour. (N) **Plate 22**

integrifolia 7 m × 4–5 m
(Coast Banksia). Sturdy character tree with short, blunt-tipped leaves, silvery below. Green-yellow cones in autumn. For sheltered and well-drained positions and coast. (N)

marginata 4 m × 3 m
(Silver Banksia). Short, narrow leaves, silver below and lemon-yellow cones from spring to early winter. Suitable for semi-shade and moist positions. Frost resistant. (N)

robur 1–2 m × 2–4 m
(Swamp Banksia). Unusual shrub with large bronze-green foliage and bronze-green cones from winter to spring. Requires moist position, preferably in sun. (N)

serrata 6 m × 4 m
(Old Man Banksia). Trunk and branches gnarled in appearance. Foliage dull green and saw-toothed, cones yellowish, autumn. Adaptable and frost resistant. (N) **Plate 23**

serratifolia 5–6 m × 4 m
(Wallum Banksia). Bright green serrated leaves and yellowish cones. Suitable for sandy soils. (Syd)

spinulosa 2 m × 3 m
(Hairpin Banksia). Dense low-growing shrub with long, narrow leaves three-toothed at apex. Brownish-red ovoid cones. Prefers well-drained soils with some moisture. Dwarf and gold forms also available. Frost resistant. (N) **Plate 24**

BARKLYA Family: Fabaceae

syringifolia 5–7 m × 3 m
Small, slow-growing, compact tree with rusty-coloured young foliage. Golden-yellow pea flowers in terminal clusters summer. For sunny position. Frost tender when young. (N)

BAUERA Family: Baueraceae

Attractive small, dense and spreading shrubs suitable for moist, shaded position. All are frost resistant.

capitata 30 cm × 1 m
Sprawling groundcover shrub with small oval foliage and pink-mauve button flowers during spring. (N) **Plate 25**

'Ruby Glow' 1 m × 1 m
(*rubioides* × *sessiliflora*). Hardy shrub with dark ruby-red flowers in spring. Suitable for most positions.

rubioides 1 × 1.5 m
(Dog Rose). Light green small leaves and pink cup-shaped flowers from spring to summer. (N)

***rubioides* White**
As above with white flowers. **Plate 26**

rubioides var. ***microphylla***
Leaves finer, habit usually prostrate. Flowers pale pink.

***rubioides* Prostrate White** 25 cm × 1 m
Hardy, low-growing shrub with pinkish-white flowers in summer.

sessiliflora 2 × 1.5 m
(Showy Bauera). Dark green hairy leaves and magenta flowers packed along upright stems in spring. (V)

BEAUFORTIA (Brush Myrtle) Family: Myrtaceae

Shrubs with papery bark and numerous small leaves. Many flowers with conspicuous stamens resembling small paint brush. Most prefer moist, sandy soils in full sun. All WA.

sparsa 2 × 1.5 m
(Swamp Brush Myrtle). Erect, lightly branching shrub with crowded oval yellowish leaves and red-orange brushes at branch tips in late summer. For warm, moist positions.

squarrosa 1–2 × 2 m
(Sand Bottlebrush). Spreading shrub with tiny crowded leaves and red flowers in large globular heads in autumn.

BILLARDIERA (Dumplings) Family: Pittosporaceae

cymosa
(Sweet Apple Berry). Shrubby, slender climber, pretty greenish-blue bell-shaped flowers during much of year but mostly in spring. Red berries. Hardy. (N)

ringens 3–5 m
Slender climbing plant with reddish stems. Clusters of rusty-orange bell flowers for long periods in spring and summer. Vigorous and hardy. For sun or semi-shade. (N) **Plate 27**

scandens
(Common Apple Berry). Slender twining shrub with light green oval foliage and yellow bells, followed by blue fruits. For semi-shade. (Syd)

BLANDFORDIA (Christmas Bells) Family: Liliaceae

nobilis 30 cm
Stiff, grass-like leaves and red-tipped large orange bell flowers in summer. Slow growing. For hot, moist positions. Frost resistant. (N) **Plate 28**

BORONIA Family: Rutaceae

Few are easy to cultivate. Leaves are strongly aromatic when crushed and pretty flowers varying in colour from white, pink, brown to blue are delightfully scented. Well-drained damp positions with a cool root run appear to suit the majority. Try planting slightly higher than level of soil, protecting stems from water rot.

anemonifolia 1 m × 60 cm
(Sticky Boronia). Light pink star flowers in spring. Frost resistant. (N)

clavata 1–1.5 m
Dense shrub with narrow, aromatic foliage and yellow flowers during winter and spring. (W)

crenulata 60 cm–1 m
Dense, small shrub with open-petalled pinkish flowers from late winter to summer. Hardy and frost tolerant. (W)

deanei 1 m
Erect-growing shrub with white to deep pink flowers. Frost resistant. (N)

denticulata 1 m × 1 m
(Mauve Boronia). Long, narrow leaves with minute teeth and flowers in loose clusters all over bush late winter to spring. Fast-growing in sun or shade. Frost resistant (N) **Plate 29**

filifolia 30 cm × 60 cm
(Slender Boronia). Low growing, open shrub with narrow foliage and pink star flowers most of year. Prefers cool but sunny position. Tolerates light frost conditions. (V)

fraseri 1.5 × 2 m
Attractive shrub with divided leaves and clustered pink flowers in spring. Requires moisture. (N)

heterophylla 1–2 m × 1 m
(Red Boronia). Compact, bushy shrub with dense dark green foliage and masses of deep red bell flowers in spring. Relatively easy. Frost resistant. (W) **Plate 30**

heterophylla* × *molloyae 1 m × 1 m
Compact, bushy shrub with cerise bell-type flowers. Considered hardier than both parents. Prefers cool root run.

megastigma 1.5 m
(Brown Boronia). Attractive shrub with fine foliage and deep purple-brown perfumed bell flowers, yellow inside. Prune hard after flowering. Short-lived, but frost resistant. (W) **Plate 31**

***megastigma* 'Lutea'** 1.5 m
Yellow flowering form, frost resistant.

microphylla 1 m × 1 m
Small, compact shrub with shiny compound leaves and rose-pink flowers in summer. (W)

mollis 1.5 m × 1.2 m
(Soft Boronia). Tall, bushy shrub with soft divided foliage and masses of bright pink flowers for long periods. Frost resistant. (N)

***mollis* 'Lorne Pride'** 1.5–2 m × 1.5 m
Dense, compact shrub with profusion of deep pink flowers. Very hardy and frost tolerant. (N) **Plate 32**

molloyae 1.5 m × 1 m
(Tall Boronia). Erect shrub with dark green, hairy, divided foliage and deep pink bell flowers. Frost resistant. (W)

muelleri 1.5 m × 1 m
(Pink Boronia). Varying in habit, this shrub has small fern-like leaves, hairy stems and pink flowers in large, open sprays. (N) **Plate 33**

pilosa 1 m × 60 cm
(Hairy Boronia). Small shrub with ferny leaves and hairy stems. Pink flowers in small clusters. For cool climates. (Tas, V)

***pilosa* 'Rose Blossom'** 50 cm × 50 cm
Highly ornamental dwarf shrub with pretty double-petalled deep pink star flowers. For semi-shade, cool positions. Prune after flowering. (V) **Plate 34**

pinnata 1–2 m × 1.2 m
Delicate shrub with much-divided leaves and rose-pink cup flowers. For well-drained soils. Frost resistant. (N)

serrulata 1 m × 60 cm
(Sydney Native Rose). Flat, rhomboidal leaves and highly perfumed deep pink terminal flowers. **Plate 35**

'Sunset Serenade' 1 m × 1 m
Hardy, compact form of *muelleri* with masses of pink star flowers in spring. Cooler positions preferred. (V) **Plate 36**

thujona 1–2 m × 1–2 m
(Bronzy Boronia). Small shrub with soft foliage and deep pink flowers in spring. Adaptable. Frost tolerant. (N)

BRACHYCHITON
Family: Sterculiaceae

acerifolium 12 × 6 m
(Flame Tree). Erect, tall tree with shiny light green lobed leaves. Partly deciduous in summer, when it bears its red flowers. Prefers deep soil and warm climate. (Syd)

populneum 10 m
(Kurrajong). Hardy and handsome tree with very variable leaves and showy white bell flowers with mottled throats in profusion in early summer.

BRACHYCOME (Daisy)
Family: Asteraceae

These are all low-growing and spreading herbs suitable for rockeries and borders. A considerable variation in leaf form is found within each species.

angustifolia
(Stiff Daisy). Narrow, light green leaves and blue-mauve daisies in spring and summer. Spreading. (N) **Plate 37**

'Break-o-Day'
Small, herbaceous plant with dark green leaves and dark blue daisy flowers most of year. For border planting.

ciliaris
Trailing plant with deeply lobed fine leaves and light mauve daisies for long periods. (V)

melanocarpa
Suckering in habit, with dark blue-green lobed foliage and large pink-mauve daisies for long periods. (N)

multifida
(Cut-leaf Daisy). Trailing plant with much divided leaves, often varying in size and shape. Mauve daisies for long periods. (N)

multifida* var. *dilatata
Suckering plant with compact foliage and mauve daisy flowers for long periods. (N)

pilliganensis
Attractive herbaceous plant with large mauve daisy flowers throughout spring and summer. (N) **Plate 38**

BRACHYSEMA Family: Fabaceae

Shrubs with alternate leaves, often silvery below and flowers of pea-type. A typical pea flower consists of five petals — an upper kidney-shaped petal, which usually embraces the other petals in the bed and is known as the *standard*; two lower petals, usually fused to form a *keel*, which can be pulled downwards to reveal the floral parts; and two side petals between the standard and the keel which are known as *wing* petals.

In Brachysema species the standard is usually very small and often inconspicuous; the wing petals fit closely to the keel, which is quite prominent.

lanceolatum 1.5 m × 2 m
(Swan River Pea). Erect shrub with dark green leaves, silvery below. Large red flowers from late winter through spring. Hardy, but requires good drainage. (W) **Plate 39**

latifolium Prostrate × 4 m
Dark green oval leaves and reddish-orange pea flowers from autumn to winter. Very vigorous, rooting at nodes. For sunny and dry positions. (W)

praemorsum Creeper × 2 m
Spreading shrub suitable as soil binder. Dark red pea flowers and fan-shaped leaves. For sunny position. (W)

sericeum to 1 m
Semi-prostrate shrub with red pea flowers and oval silvery leaves. Adaptable. (W)

sericeum* var. *angustifolium Prostrate × 1.5 m
Mainly prostrate plant with cream flowers, narrow foliage. Hardy. (W)

BUCKINGHAMIA Family: Proteaceae

celsissima 6 m × 3 m
(Ivory Curl Flower). Large shrub or small tree, large dark green leaves very variable when young. Pendulous spikes of cream flowers during summer and autumn. Ideal specimen or street tree. (Q)

BULBINE Family: Liliaceae

bulbosa
Onion-like herb with yellow flowers in spring and summer. (N)

CALLICOMA Family: Cunoniaceae

serratifolia 6 m × 3 m
(Black Wattle). Small tree with large dark green serrated leaves, shiny above and woolly below. Large yellow ball flowers in spring. For rich, moist position. (N)

CALLISTEMON (Bottlebrush) Family: Myrtaceae

Shrubs and trees with tough leathery entire leaves and bark which is often papery. Flowers are dense terminal spikes in which the stamens are long and conspicuous, giving the flower its 'colour'. Very hardy, they are suitable for over-wet to well-drained positions. Prune behind flowers after flowering to keep plants bushy.

brachyandrus 3.5–5 × 3 m
Needle-shaped foliage and red brushes tipped gold. Very hardy. Frost resistant. (N)

'Burgundy' 2–3 m × 2–3 m
(*citrinus* form). Medium shrub of rounded habit, dense to ground. Flat lanceolate deep green leaves. Medium to large burgundy brushes during spring and summer. **Plate 40**

'Candy Pink' 2 m × 2 m
(sp. *guyra*? form). Medium shrub with lanceolate light green foliage. Masses of pink flowers during late spring and autumn. **Plate 41**

'Captain Cook' 1–1.5 m × 1.5 m
A dwarf hardy shrub with lanceolate weeping foliage. Masses of short red brushes throughout the year, but mainly during spring. Can be successfully grown in pots. **Plate 42**

citrinus 2.5–3 m × 4 m
Hardy shrub with stiff lanceolate foliage and red to crimson brushes from spring to autumn. Suitable any position. Coastal

***citrinus* 'Eastland'** 2 m × 1.5 m
Small shrub with stiff foliage and soft pink new growth. large bright pink-mauve bottlebrush flowers in spring.

***citrinus* 'White'** 1 m × 2 m
Low-growing, compact form with soft green new foliage and white bottlebrush flowers spring and autumn. Very hardy. **Plate 43**

comboynensis 1.5–3 × 2 m
Medium-sized shrub with showy scarlet brushes. Suitable for warm, moist positions and any soil type.

'Dawson River' 6–10 m × 4 m
(*viminalis* form). Slender weeping tree with large crimson flower spikes. Tolerates moist soils and slight frosts. Prefers full sun. **Plate 44**

'Demesne Rowena' 2 m × 2 m
Small to medium rounded shrub with flat semi-stiff lanceolate leaves and large pink-mauve bottlebrush flowers in clusters during spring and autumn. Hardy and suitable most positions. **Plate 46**

'Endeavour' 4 × 2 m
(*citrinus* form). Medium to tall shrub with flat and large green leaves. Large red brushes, often borne in clusters, during early spring and autumn.

'Eureka' 3–4 m × 2 m
Tall growing, upright shrub with long lanceolate foliage. Small mauve-red flowers during early summer.

'Hannah Ray' 4 m × 2 m
(*viminalis* form). Small tree of strong weeping habit. Long crimson brush flowers for long periods spring and autumn.

'Harkness' 4 m × 3 m
(*viminalis* hybrid). Attractive small tree with partly weeping habit. Huge long red brushes spring and autumn. For coastal planting. May take couple of years to bloom profusely. (SA) **Plate 45**

'Kings Park Special' 5 m × 3 m
Small compact, weeping tree with large red bottlebrush flowers in spring. Excellent specimen or street-planting tree. Extremely hardy. **Plate 47**

linearis 3 m × 2.5 m
(Narrow-leaf Bottlebrush). Bushy shrub with long, thin, sharply pointed leaves and red brushes. For coastal and dry areas. (N)

'Little John' 1 m × 1 m
Dark green lanceolate foliage. Dark red brushes in spring. Excellent rockery specimen. **Plate 48**

'Mauve Mist' 2–3 m × 3 m
(*citrinus* form). Dense shrub with silvery new growth and mauve bottlebrush flowers in clusters, mostly in spring. **Plate 49**

'Mt Oberon' 1.5 m × 2 m
Evergreen, small shrub with attractive silvery new foliage and large yellow bottlebrush flowers in late winter. Hardy for most positions. (V) **Plate 50**

pallidus 3–4 m × 4 m
(Lemon Bottlebrush). Attractive shrub with yellow brushes tinged pink. Suitable for coastal planting and snow areas. Frost resistant. (V, Tas)

pachyphyllus 1 m × 1.5 m
Open shrub with long narrow leaves and red or green bottlebrush flowers during spring and summer. Suitable for most soils and positions. (N)

***paludosus* 'Father Christmas'** 2–3 m × 2.5 m
(Swamp Bottlebrush). Upright shrub with pale pink or cream sparse brushes, spring to summer. Very hardy. (N)

phoeniceus 2 m × 2.5 m
(Fiery Bottlebrush). Attractive spreading shrub with brilliant red brushes late spring. Appreciates summer watering. Suited to warm, heavy soils, coast and frost areas. (W)

***phoeniceus* 'Pink Ice'** 2 m × 2 m
Dense shrub with blue-green foliage and true pink brushes with white tips during spring. Salt tolerant. **Plate 51**

pinifolius 2–4 × 1–2 m
(Green Bottlebrush). Narrow, stiff foliage and large green brushes. For sunny, moist position. Also frost resistant. (N) **Plate 52**

polandii 2–3 m × 2.5 m
Bushy, densely hairy plant with rich bronze new foliage. Deep red brushes in spring. Hardy, but slightly frost tender. Prefers moist position. (Q)

'Prolific' 4 m × 2 m
(*viminalis* form). Bright green foliage and masses of bright red bottlebrush flowers during early summer. **Plate 53**

'Reeves Pink' 2–3 × 2 m
(*citrinus* form). Much-branched shrub with pink bottlebrush flower clusters in spring and autumn. **Plate 54**

'Rose Opal' 2.5–2 m
(*viminalis* form). Dwarf weeping shrub with deep red flowers fading to rose pink, usually borne in clusters, most prolific in spring.

salignus 5 m × 2.5 m
(Pink Tips). Bushy, weeping shrub with attractive pink new growth. Pale lemon brushes late spring. Suitable for coast, moist or dry conditions. Red flowering form also available. Frost resistant. (N) **Plate 55**

***salignus* 'Rubra'**
Red flowering form.

sieberi 2 × 2 m
Dense shrub with narrow, prickly foliage and yellow brushes in summer. Frost resistant. (N)

speciosus 3 × 3 m
(Showy Bottlebrush). Magnificent shrub with thick, narrow leaves, prominent midrib and margin. Long red brushes, gold-tipped. Any position. (W)

subulatus 1–1.5 m × 1.5 m
Small bushy plant with fine leaves. Compact small dark red brushes in spring. Prefers moist position. (N)

'Tinaroo' 3 m × 2 m
(unnamed species). Medium to tall shrub with silky new growth and dense, dark red flower spikes. Very hardy, tolerating dry and cold conditions.

viminalis 6 × 4 m
(Weeping Bottlebrush). Gracefully weeping small tree with long-lasting red brushes in spring. For moist conditions. Slightly frost tender.

A number of forms are available in cultivation.

'Violaceus' 2.5–3 m
Attractive shrub with smooth thin leaves, thick at margins and sharp pointed. Purple brushes in spring. (N) **Plate 56**

'Western Glory' 2–4 m × 2 m
(*citrinus* hybrid). Medium shrub with mauve-red flowers in spring. Suitable for sun or semi-shade. **Plate 57**

CALLITRIS (Cypress Pine)
Family: Cupressaceae

Australian conifers represented by some 15 species, all preferring sunny, well-drained position. White-ant resistant and cone-bearing.

columellaris 8–10 m × 3 m
Upright, symmetrical tree with blue-green foliage. Slow growing, suitable for sandy soils. (N)

preissii 10 m
Slender olive foliage, narrow habit. For dry position. (N)

macleayana 5 × 3 m
Stringy bark, spreading foliage. (N)

rhomboidea 5–8 m × 3 m
(Port Jackson Cypress). Upright, small tree with narrow habit and attractive pendulous new growth. (N)

CALOCEPHALUS
Family: Compositae

brownii 50 cm × 2 m
(Cushion/Snow Bush). White woolly bush with compact, tangled narrow leaves and yellowish ball flowers at ends of stems in spring and summer. Open, well-drained position required, but salt, drought and frost tolerant. (SA, Tas, V, W)

CALOSTEMMA
Family: Amaryllidaceae

purpureum 30 cm × 30 cm
(Garland Lily). Long, erect, shiny dark-green leaves and red-purple funnel-shaped flowers in summer to autumn. Suitable for rockeries. Hardy, tolerating moist to dry soils in sunny position. (N)

CALOTHAMNUS (Net Bush)
Family: Myrtaceae

Useful shrubs for hot, dry regions, resistant to salty sea winds. Flowers are reddish one-sided 'bottlebrushes', usually deep within bush on older wood, and attractive to birds. Prune after flowering. All WA.

gilesii 1.5–2.5 × 2 m
Sharp pointed pine-like foliage and scarlet flowers late spring. Suitable for exposed position, and frost resistant.

quadrifidus 2 × 2 m
(One-sided Bottlebrush). Dense, multi-branched shrub with hairy, dark green, pine-like leaves and red brushes in spring. Frost resistant.

***quadrifidus* prostrate** 60 cm × 2 m
Low spreading form. Very hardy.

sanguineus 2 m
Bushy shrub with needle leaves and claw-like blood-red flowers late spring to winter. Keep pruned. For sunny positions.

villosus 1.5 × 1 m
Greyish woolly needle leaves, densely on stems. Red flowers from late spring to winter. For sunny positions. Frost resistant.

CALYTRIX (Fringe Myrtle)
Family: Myrtaceae

alpestris 1 m × 1 m
(Snow Myrtle). Compact shrub with fine foliage and white star flowers from pink buds. For moist, semi-shaded positions. (SA, V)

sullivanii 1.5 m
Fresh, green, compact foliage and masses of starry flowers in spring. Sunny, well-drained position. Frost resistant. (V)

tetragona 1.5 m × 1.2 m
(Common Fringe Myrtle). Upright to drooping shrub with crowded small leaves and white or pink flowers covering bush in spring. Warm, well-drained position. Frost resistant. (N)

CARPOBROTUS Family: Aizoaceae

***modestus* Prostrate** × 2 m
(Inland Pigface). Succulent trailer with red and grey leaves. Purple to magenta daisies. Spring and summer. (N)

CASSIA Family: Fabaceae

artemisioides 2 × 2 m
(Silver Cassia). Bushy shrub with pinnate silvery foliage and bright yellow buttercup flowers in spring. Well-drained soils, including heavy soils and coastal positions. (N)

nemophila 2 m × 2 m
(Desert Cassia). Finely divided yellowish-green leaflets and

small clusters of yellow flowers. For warm, dry positions. (N)

odorata 1 m × 1 m
Shrub with bright green compound leaves and yellow buttercup flowers. Suitable moist positions. (N) **Plate 58**

CASTANOSPERMUM
Family: Fabaceae

australe 20 m
(Black Bean). Fine spreading tree with smooth grey trunk and large glossy divided leaves. Pea flowers somewhat fleshy, yellow to orange-red in sprays. Thin pea pods and large 'chestnut' seeds. May take several years to flower. (N)

CASUARINA (She-Oak)
Family: Casuarinaceae

Shrubs and trees with jointed branchlets and leaves reduced to scale-like teeth around the joints. Flowers unisexual. Fruit a winged nut. Very adaptable. Suitable host for epiphytic orchids.

cunninghamiana 20 m × 7.5 m
(River Oak). Dense branches, fine leaves and very small red flowers followed by small cones. Most adaptable, suited to clay soils and for windbreak planting. Frost resistant. (N)

distyla 1.5–2 × 2 m
Dwarf species. Extremely hardy, for coastal or clay positions. (N)

equisetifolia 2–3 m × 6 m
(Horse-tail Casuarina). Small tree with weeping grey foliage. Suited for coast. Hardy. (N)

glauca 8 m × 2 m
(Swamp Oak). Fine greyish leaves and flakey bark. Barrel cones. Suitable for shade, swamp or coast and as windbreak. (N)

littoralis 6 × 4.5 m
(Black She-Oak). Upright species with dark green branches. Suited to any well-drained position. (N)

nana 2 m × 2 m
Densely branching shrub. Extremely hardy. (N)

stricta 5–7 m × 4.5 m
(Drooping She-Oak). Beautiful little tree with weeping branches and large oval cones. Hardy. (V)

torulosa 6 m × 4.5 m
(Rose She-Oak). Pyramid-shaped ornamental tree with rough furrowed bark and drooping fine reddish branchlets and leaves. For open, moist position. (N)

CERATOPETALUM
Family: Cunoniaceae

gummiferum 6 m × 3 m
Shrub or small tree with rough brownish bark and shiny leaves, bronzed at tips. White flowers turning red in summer. Moist, open position. Also variegated form. (N) **Plate 59**

CHAMELAUCIUM (Waxflower)
Family: Myrtaceae

uncinatum 2 m × 2 m
(Geraldton Wax). Spreading shrub with narrow needle foliage and large waxy flowers in spring. For warm, sandy soils. Do not over-water. Cut back hard after flowering. (W) **Plate 60**

uncinatum **'Purple Pride'**
As for above, except that flowers are dark red or burgundy in colour. **Plate 61**

uncinatum **'University Red'** 2 m × 2 m
Spreading shrub with weeping needle foliage and dark red flowers in spring. Prune hard after flowering. (W) **Plate 62**

uncinatum **'White'**
As for *uncinatum* except flowers are white. **Plate 63**

CHORIZEMA (Flame Pea)
Family: Fabaceae

cordatum 50 cm × 1 m
Bushy shrub with many slender spikes of orange/red or yellow pea flowers in spring. Adaptable, but requires to be cut back hard after flowering. (W) **Plate 64**

diversifolium
Light climber with twining branches and variable leaves. Excellent basket specimen. Orange and yellow flowers in summer. (W)

CISSUS Family: Vitaceae

antarctica climber or ground cover
(Kangaroo Vine). Glossy, heart-shaped, serrated foliage,

rusty coloured when new. Very fast growing, climbing by tendrils. Tolerates shade and suitable for indoors. (N)

hypoglauca prostrate or climbing
Vigorous woody, tendril climber with woolly rust-coloured new growth. Yellow flowers in summer followed by blue-black berries. Suitable for shady positions.

CLEMATIS Family: Ranunculaceae

aristata climber
(Old Man's Beard). Strong growing woody climber or ground cover. Light green leaflets, irregularly toothed, on long stalks. Masses of white star flowers in summer, followed by cotton-like fruits. For sheltered, moist and shady positions. (N) **Plate 65**

microphylla climber
Light climber with divided foliage and white star flowers followed by attractive woolly seeds. For semi-shade and coastal positions. (N)

CLIANTHUS Family: Fabaceae

formosus prostrate × 2 m
(Sturt's Desert Pea). Trailing mat plant with divided grey-green leaves. Spectacular crimson glossy flowers after rain. For light sandy well-drained soils in sunny position. Coast or inland. Treat as an annual. (N)

CONOSTYLIS Family: Amaryllidaceae

aculeata
(Cone Flower). Perennial clump with woolly yellow flowers in spring. Well-drained position. (W)

seorsiflora
Perennial tuft with yellow star flowers deep in clump. (W)

stylidioides
Perennial clump with yellow star flowers on long stems. (W)

CORDYLINE Family: Agavaceae

stricta 2.5 m
Palm-like plant with large leaves and spikes of light blue or pink flowers. Suitable for sheltered position or tub. (N)

CORREA Family: Rutaceae

Most of the species require cool, well-drained positions. All have bell-shaped flowers, varying in shape from open to long, thin, closed bells. Most bloom for long periods in the year.

aemula 1 × 1 m
(Hairy Correa). Bushy shrub with hairy foliage and green bells in spring. (V)

alba 1 × 2 m
Attractive rounded grey-green leaves and white flowers with spreading petals in winter. Tough, frost and salt resistant, suitable for sun or semi-shade. (N)

backhousiana 1–2 m × 1.5 m
Dark green oval foliage and cream bells in spring. Frost resistant. (Tas)

baeuerlenii 1 m × 60 cm
(Chef's Cap Correa). Erect shrub with lance-like leaves and long tubular yellow bells in winter. For semi-shade, moist positions. (N)

calycina 1.2 × 1.5 m
Woolly foliage and greenish bells winter to spring. (SA)

decumbens Prostrate × 1 m
Small, narrow, dark green leaves and thin, upturned tubular red bells with green tips for most of year. Frost tolerant and hardy. (SA)

'Dusky Bells' 60 cm × 60 cm
Lush oval foliage and deep pink flowers in autumn. **Plate 66**

glabra 1 m × 1 m
Spreading shrub with deep green leaves and green flowers in winter. (V)

lawrenciana 3 × 1.5 m
(Tree Correa). Tall, narrow habit, leathery foliage. Cream or red flowers from winter to spring. For shade, moist. (Tas, V)

'Mannii' 1 m
(*pulchella* × *reflexa*). Compact shrub with oval leaves and salmon-red bells from autumn to winter. Frost resistant. (SA)

'Marian's Marvel' 1 m × 1 m
(*reflexa* × *backhousiana*). Very hardy small shrub with oval foliage and attractive pink and cream bell flowers from autumn through winter. **Plate 67**

pulchella 30 cm
Small shrub with concave, heart-shaped leaves and salmon-coloured tubular flowers in winter. Coastal. (SA)

reflexa to 1.5 m × 1 m
Many forms found, with leaves varying from oval to linear.

Flowers usually red and hanging with green or yellow tips. Coastal. (N)

***reflexa* 'Salmon'** 60 cm × 1 m
A superb small growing hardy shrub suitable for most soils and positions. Green oval foliage and salmon-pink flowers from late summer through autumn.

***reflexa* 'Squat'** 30 cm × 30 cm
Small growing shrub suitable for rockery planting. Red and yellow bell-shaped flowers late winter. (N)

reflexa* var. *nummulariifolia 30 cm × 1 m
Small shrub with attractive rounded foliage and small red bell flowers. Hardy and tolerant of coastal situation. (N)

CROWEA Family: Rutaceae

Useful and beautiful shrubs which require cool, well-drained positions.

exalata 1.5 m × 1.2 m
Small plant with narrow leaves and bright pink star flowers along stems in summer and autumn. Hardy, suiting open, sunny positions. (N)

exalata* × *saligna 1 m × 1 m
Small shrub with narrow leaves and masses of large pink star flowers during spring and autumn. Requires good soil and cool position **Plate 68**

saligna 1 × 1 m
Light, narrow foliage and very large waxy pink flowers in spring and at other times. Less hardy, requiring deep soil, moisture. Jan–July. (N)

'Poorinda Ecstasy' 1–1.5 m
Attractive shrub with iridescent pink flowers many times a year. Hardy.

CRYPTANDRA Family: Rhamnaceae

amara to 1 m × 30 cm
Small clustered leaves on interlacing branches, tiny cream waxy fragrant cream bells in spring. (N)

DAMPIERA Family: Goodeniaceae

Small, mostly prostrate plants which require open, sunny positions but protection from the hottest part of the day. Some moisture.

cuneata Spreads to 1 m
Suckering plant with blue flowers winter to summer, withstands drought and prefers sandy soils. (W)

diversifolia Spreading to 1 m
Compact growing with small leaves and suckering habit. Brilliant blue flowers most of year, but best from winter to spring. For moist, warm, open position with well-drained light soils. (W) **Plate 69**

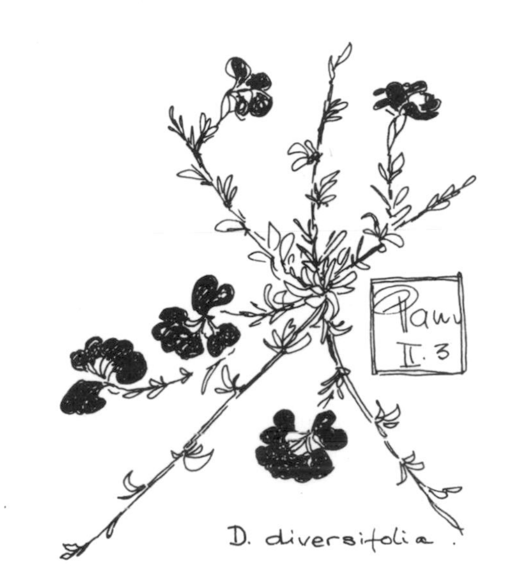

hederacea Spreading to 1 m
Low-trailing plant with ivy-like leaves and pale purple-blue flowers in spring. Prefers moist conditions. (W)

stricta Spreading to 30 cm
Flat, stiff leaves and light blue flowers on erect stems from spring to summer. Scrambling. Frost resistant. (N)

trigona Spreading to 60 cm
Long, almost grassy stems with tiny leaves and profusion of blue flowers in spring. **Plate 70**

DARWINIA Family: Myrtaceae

citriodora 1 × 1.2 m
(Lemon-scented Myrtle). Narrow, pointed, red-bronze tipped, grey-green foliage. Small, tightly packed red and yellow flowers in spring. For sunny position. (W) **Plate 71**

fascicularis 1 × 1 m
(Tufted Darwinia). Fine grey tufted foliage and red-green flowers in spring. Very hardy. Frost resistant. (N)

grandiflora 1.2 × 1 m
Fine light green foliage and large pink flowers in winter. For moist, well-drained position. (N) **Plate 72**

homoranthoides 60 cm × 1 m
Particularly attractive greenish-pink foliage and somewhat insignificant flowers which give the whole bush a yellow top in spring. For sunny position. Frost resistant. (V) **Plate 73**

oldfieldii 30 cm × 60 cm
Spreading shrub with red-purple flowers late winter. (W)

procera 2 m × 1 m
Neat, upright shrub with attractive foliage and clusters of white flowers, aging to red, in spring and summer. For partially shaded position. (N)

rhadinophylla 60 cm + 1 m
Diffuse, almost prostrate shrub with red flowers in spring. For well-drained, semi-shade positions. (W)

taxifolia prostrate
Attractive small plant with slightly fleshy leaves and pale pink flowers in spring-summer. Suitable for well-drained sunny spot, inland or coast. (N)

DIANELLA Family: Liliaceae

revoluta 20 cm × 30 cm
Leaves almost flat, dull blue-green with bluish lustre, flowers held high, followed by blue berries. Frost resistant. (N)

tasmanica 1 m × 50 cm
Heavy strap-like foliage, deep blue flowers with yellow centres, purple berries. Frost resistant. (N)

DILLWYNIA (Parrot Pea) Family: Fabaceae

juniperina 1 m × 60 cm
Dense shrub with sharp, small needle leaves and yellow-brown pea flowers in small clusters in spring. (N)

retorta 30–50 cm × 60 cm
(Eggs & Bacon). Leaves twisted and hairless, flowers yellow, often with red centre, in spring. (Syd)

DIPLARRENA Family: Iridaceae

moraea 30 cm × 30 cm
(Butterfly Flag). Narrow, dark, rush-like leaves. White iris-type flowers tinged yellow and mauve and held on long, slender stems. Suitable for sunny rockeries. Frost resistant. (N)

DODONAEA (Hop Bush) Family: Sapindaceae

viscosa 3 m × 2 m
(Giant Hopbush). Tall shrub with sticky, shiny leaves and three-winged red-purple hops. For well-drained, sunny position. Frost resistant. (N)

DORYANTHES Family: Agavaceae

excelsa 2–3 m
(Gymea Lily). Sword-like foliage up to 2 m long, light green in colour. Red flowers on long stems in globular heads. For coastal positions. Suitable for tubs. (N)

ELAEOCARPUS Family: Elaeocarpaceae

reticulatus 3–5 m × 3 m
(Blueberry Ash). Small tree wth straight, smooth trunk and grey bark. Leaves elliptical and toothed, often rusty at tips. Flowers delicate white bells followed by blue berries. Pink form also available. For moist positions, but frost resistant. (N) **Plate 74**

EPACRIS (Heath) Family: Epacridaceae

impressa 1 m × 60 cm
(Pink Heath). Sprawling heath shrub with dark green, sharp-pointed foliage and bell flowers most of year. White, red or pink forms available. For sunny, well-drained position. Frost resistant. (N) **Plate 75**

microphylla 30–100 cm × 30 cm
Fine leaves and small white spring flowers. Any well-drained position. (N)

longiflora 1 × 1 m
(Fuchsia Heath). Leaves tapering and sharp pointed. Tubular flowers, rich red with white tips, most of year. Warm, semi-shade position. (Syd)

pulchella 1–2 m × 30 cm
Slender-growing heath with sharp-pointed foliage and white or pink star flowers packed at tops of stems. Frost resistant. (N)

EREMOPHILA (Emu-bush)
Family: Myoporaceae

The majority of the species come from Western Australia and are hot inland shrubs requiring dry conditions and sun. Flowers are mostly tubular.

divaricata 1 m
Fine grey foliage and mauve flowers in winters. (N)

gibbifolia 1 × 1 m
Leaves tiny, warty and pressed against stems. Lilac-blue flowers for long periods. (SA)

glabra 1 × 1 m
Very many forms of this shrub. Most have fairly large orange-red flowers in late spring. Suitable for coastal planting, and frost resistant. (N)

laanii 1.5–3 m
Much branched shrub with light green leaves and deep pink flowers in spring.

maculata 1–1.2 m × 1 m
(Spotted Emu-Bush). Many forms available. Most have narrow leaves and red flowers, spotted inside. Yellow form also available.Suitable for coastal planting. Frost resistant. (N)

ERIOSTEMON (Wax Flower)
Family: Rutaceae

australasius 1.5–2 m × 1 m
Thick lanceolate leaves and large pink waxy star flowers in spring. Well-drained, sunny position. (N) **Plate 76**

difformis 30 cm–1 m × 1.2 m
Low-spreading dainty shrub with white starry flowers, pink in bud. Leaves short, narrow and slightly warty. (N)

myoporoides 1–2 m × 1.5 m
(Long-leaf Waxflower). Rounded shrub with slender, long leaves and white flowers pink in bud, mostly in spring and summer. Frost resistant. Suitable for sun or shade. (N) **Plate 77**

***myoporoides* 'Profusion'** 1–2 m × 1.5 m
Similar in form to above but with shorter oval leaves and masses of white star flowers in spring and summer. For sun or shade, tolerates frost. (V)

nodiflorus 50 cm × 30 cm
Small-growing shrub with fine foliage and pink star flowers clustered up stems in spring. (W) **Plate 78**

'Stardust' 1 m
Attractive hybrid with short oval leaves and a mass of white star flowers in leaf axils for long periods, spring. Hardy.

verrucosus 1–1.5 m × 60 cm
(Fairy Waxflower). Small, broad, blunt, warty foliage and stems. Flowers white from pink buds in spring. (N)

EUCALYPTUS (Gum Tree)
Family: Myrtaceae

There are approximately 400 species found only in Australia and a few neighbouring islands. They are found as trees or mallees. A mallee is a small species with a number of thin stems arising from a woody base or lignotuber. In cultivation, however, mallee species often form only one stem. Bark is varied in texture and colour, but typical in each species, and often used as a means of identification. The leaves are nearly always characteristically aromatic. Juvenile leaves are often replaced by quite different adult leaves, making identification from leaves difficult. Flower colour is given by the numerous stamens. In the bud stage the flower consists of a lower floral tube and an upper cap (*operculum*). The cap, which replaces the petals and sepals, falls off when ripe to 'release' the stamens. Fruits, known as 'gum nuts', are also typical for any species, but vary greatly.

In the following descriptions flower colour is only given where this is *not* cream or white. Heights indicated should be considered as relative rather than accurate. The final height of a tree is dependent upon soil and climatic conditions and is often very different in cultivation from the natural habit. A *Eucalypt* growing to 30 m in ideal conditions may, for example, only achieve 10 m in poor conditions such as the Hawkesbury sandstone country.

archeri to 60 m
(Alpine Cedar Gum). Small tree with smooth white bark, turning grey-brown before shedding in strips. Suitable for cold climates. (T)

blakelyi to 20 m × 6 m
Short, beautifully mottled trunk. Large spreading crown and drooping branchlets. Extremely hardy, frost resistant. (N)

botryoides to 20 m × 8 m
(Bangalay). Furrowed bark and thick crown. Rapid growing, hardy shade-giving tree. Salt tolerant. (N)

caesia 4–6 m × 8 m
(Gungurru). Open-textured tree with smooth deep brown bark, peeling to cream. Rose-pink flower clusters followed by mealy-grey nuts. (W)

***calophylla* 'Rosea'** 5–6 m × 3 m
Moderately fast-growing tree with thick crown and pink to red flowers. Frost hardy. (W)

camaldulensis to 20 m
(River Red Gum). Inland species with smooth grey bark streaked red. Dense crown. Fast growing. Drought and frost resistant. (N)

cinerea 12 m × 10 m
(Argyle Apple). Short trunk covered with rugged red-brown fibrous bark. Compact dense crown of silvery oval juvenile leaves which persist for some time. Responds to training. Relatively slow growing. Drought and frost hardy. (N)

curtisii to 7 m
(Plunkett Mallee). Slender-stemmed mallee or small tree with smooth bark shedding in strips to white. Hardy, frost resistant and very floriferous. (Q)

citriodora 20 m × 10 m
(Lemon-scented Gum). Most graceful tree with white bark and open crown producing only light shade. Very hardy. Winter flowering. (Q)

***cladocalyx* 'Nana'** 4–5 m
(Dwarf Sugar Gum). Excellent windbreak species of bushy habit. Deep glossy green rounded leaves. Relatively drought tolerant. Hardy and fast growing. (SA)

crebra to 25 m × 6 m
(Narrow-leaved Ironbark). Very hardy and tolerant tree with hard grey furrowed bark, deeply impregnated with reddish gum. Leaves narrow, dull grey-green. Flowers winter to summer. (N)

elata 10–15 m × 15 m
(Willow Peppermint). Bark rough, often rectangularly cracked at base and smooth white above. Crown of long narrow drooping leaves providing light shade. Masses of flowers. Frost hardy. (N) **Plate 79**

erythrocorys to 8 m × 3 m
(Illyarrie). Adaptable tree with unusual red bud caps opening to yellow flowers. (W)

eximia to 15 m × 9 m
(Yellow Bloodwood). Scaly, yellow-brown bark and irregular crown. Large flowers, very occasionally yellow. For poor soils and coastal planting. (N)

fibrosa 15 m × 4 m
(Broad-leaved Red Ironbark). Erect, spreading tree with dark brown bark. Extremely hardy in most soils and suitable for coastal planting. (N)

ficifolia to 19 m × 4.5 m
(WA Scarlet Flowering Gum). Small rough-barked tree with dense round head and scarlet flowers in summer. Prefers coastal soils (W)

forrestiana 3–5 m × 4 m
(Fuchsia Gum). Smooth grey or brown bark. Attractive red flower buds and yellow stamens. Drought and frost resistant. Suitable also for coastal planting. (W) **Plate 80**

globulus 'compacta' to 15 m
(Tasmanian Blue Gum). Extremely rapid smaller growing form with blue juvenile foliage contrasting attractively with long leathery adult leaves at its transition stage. Flowers singly in spring. Prefers moist heavy soils. Frost hardy. (Tas)

globulus* ssp. *bicostata to 30 m
(Southern Blue Gum). Similar, but flowers borne in groups of three in winter. Rough barked at base, smooth and bluish higher. Suitable for frost areas. (N)

gummifera to 20 m × 6 m
(Red Bloodwood). Persistent irregularly cracked brown bark. Dense crown of dark green leaves. Suitable for coast and windbreak planting. (N)

gunnii to 18 m
(Cider Gum). Tall tree with smooth grey-orange bark. Round, bluish juvenile foliage. Flowers in summer. (T)

haemastoma 5–7 m × 6 m
(Scribbly Gum). Small, slow-growing tree with light irregular crown and attractive white trunk often marked by insect scribbles. Will grow in extremely infertile soils, but requires good drainage. (N) **Plate 81**

lansdowneana 4–5 m × 3 m
(Purple Mallee Box). Mallee or small tree with drooping branches. Bark rough and flaky at base, smooth grey above. Relatively fast growing. Flowers pink to purple in summer. Drought and frost resistant. (A)

lehmanni 6–10 m × 6 m
(Bushy Yate). Dense round bushy tree, branching from near ground level. Frost, salt and drought resistant. Winter flowering. (N)

***leucoxylon* 'Rosea'** 5–9 m × 4.5 m
Slender tree with rough bark and drooping smooth bluish branches. Large open crown, varied flowering time and colour. Often pink. (N) **Plate 82**

leucoxylon* var. *macrocarpa 5–9 m × 4 m
As above, but larger flowering form, mostly red flowers.

luehmanniana 6 m
(Yellow-top Ash). Found on shallow infertile soils as a mallee. Huge broad juvenile leaves. Suitable for cool, damp sites subject to drying out as in Sydney area. (N)

maculata to 10 m
(Spotted Gum). Long, straight, mottled trunk which changes colour. Found on coastal strip, but is very hardy, drought and frost resistant. (N)

mannifera* ssp. *maculosa to 10 m × 12 m
Excellent graceful cool climate tree, rapid growing when

young. Smooth white bark turning pink through red in summer. Light shade provider. (N)

melliodora 20–30 m × 12 m
(Yellow Box). Bark yellow-brown on trunk and larger branches, grading to smooth white, cream or grey on smaller branches. Good shade-providing crown. Honey-scented flowers in summer. Frost resistant. (N)

microcorys to 20 m × 4.5 m
(Tallowwood). Height variable. Brown bark, attractive soft light green foliage, often mauve when young. Tolerant of shade. For clay soils and coastal conditions. (N)

moluccana to 20 m
(Coastal Grey Box). Upright branching tree with moderately dense crown. Rough grey bark shed in long strips from above. For heavy clay soils. (N)

nicholii to 20 m × 8.5 m
(Narrow-leaved Black Peppermint). Fast-growing tree with dark furrowed bark, rounded compact crown and fine bluish leaves, often plum-tinted when young. Frost resistant. (N)

paniculata to 30 m
(Grey Ironbark). Dark green furrowed bark impregnated with red gum. Long dark green leaves, paler below. Summer flowers. For any soil types. (N)

parramattensis 12 m
Smooth blotched deciduous bark. For poor sandy soils. (N)

pauciflora 7 m
(Snow Gum). Cold country species with short, curved trunk, smooth bark often blotched yellow and marked by insect scribbles. Summer flowering. Frost tolerant. (N)

perriniana to 7 m
(Spinning Gum). All foliage grey in colour with stems passing through centres of juvenile leaves. When dead these tend to spin. This foliage renewed by lopping. Cold climate species often found on wet soils. (N)

pilularis to 30 m
(Blackbutt). Straight trunk, finely fibrous at base and smooth higher. Open crown. Summer flowers. Fast growing, suitable for coastal gardens. (N)

piperita 10 m
(Sydney Peppermint). Short trunk with rough fibrous bark and wide-spreading branches. Suitable for cool areas. (N)

polyanthemos to 15 m
(Red Box). Short trunk, irregular shade-producing crown of grey-green leaves. Juvenile foliage circular and blue-grey in colour. Moderately drought and frost hardy. Lizard-skin bark. (N)

preissiana to 3–3.5 m
(Bell Fruit Mallee). Straggly mallee with smooth or mottled grey bark and thick leaves. Yellowish flowers followed by large ball-shaped fruits. (W)

pulchella 8 m
(White Peppermint). Smooth white bark above scaly base. Light crown of fine bluish leaves. For cool moist climates. Frost and snow tolerant. (Tas)

punctata 10 m
(Grey Gum). Extremely adaptable. Very variable in height. Bark smooth grey and pink, crown dense. (N)

robusta 16 m
(Swamp Mahogany). Spreading tree with thick growth of dark glossy leaves. Coarse fibrous bark. Fast growing, suitable for coast and moist soils. (N)

saligna 30 m
(Sydney Blue Gum). Bark smooth and grey except at base. Very fast growing. Summer flowering. (N)

scoparia to 10 m
(Willow Gum). Slender tree with white trunk and long narrow drooping foliage. Summer flowers. (N)

sideroxylon 'Rosea' 10 m
(Ironbark). Very dark black bark with contrasting soft grey-green foliage. Flower colour varies from pink through red. Extremely hardy. Frost tolerant. (N) **Plate 83**

spathulata to 8 m
(Swamp Mallee). Elegant mallee. Smooth shining bronzed bark. Moderately drought and frost tolerant. Suitable for heavy soils. (W)

stricta to 5 m
Hardy small tree, often of mallee form. Cream flowers in summer and autumn. Suitable for most positions.

tereticornis 20 m
(Forest Red Gum). May require staking and pruning when young. Grey-barked, blotched black, ribboning from upper branches. Fast growing and suitable for clay soils. (N)

torelliana to 20 m
(Cadaga). Tall growing tree with large hairy leaves and green smooth bark. Tolerates extremes of temperature including light frosts and high rainfall. Coastal. (Q)

torquata to 8 m
(Coral Gum). Rough grey bark, sometimes fissured, but smooth higher on trunk. Spreading crown. Flowers pale pink to red in summer, often in second year. (W)

viminalis 10–15 m
(Manna Gum). Smooth white trunk, peeling in dark ribbons from upper branches. Suitable for heavy soils with plenty of moisture and frost resistant. (N)

viridis 2–6 m
(Green Mallee). Slender, flexible mallee. Suitable as sand binder and for clay soils. (N)

woodwardii 10 m
(Lemon-flowered Gum). Smooth white-barked tree for dry inland. Clusters of yellow flowers from young age. (W)

EUGENIA Family: Myrtaceae

wilsonii 3–4 × 2 m
Spectacular small tree with glossy leaves, reddish when young. Fluffy crimson flowers followed by white fruits. Benefits from regular watering and general fertiliser. (Q) **Plate 84**

EUTAXIA Family: Fabaceae

cuneata 30 cm × 30 cm
Small growing plant with solitary orange pea-type flowers from winter to early spring. For light soils in open positions. (W)

obovata 1.5–2 m × 2 m
Leaves in four racks up stem, with yellow and red pea flowers packed at tops of branches from spring for long periods. For sunny, well-drained position. (W)

FRANKENIA Family: Frankeniaceae

pauciflora Prostrate × 1 m
(Common Sea Heath). Dense mat plant with light grey-green small leaves and delicate pink cup flowers late summer. Salt and frost resistant. (W)

GOODENIA Family: Goodeniaceae

hederacea Prostrate × 1 m
Leaves variable, usually ivy-like, rooting at nodes. Yellow fan flowers for long periods. Frost tolerant. (N)

lanata Prostrate × 1 m
Clump of thick blunt leaves and trailing stems. Dark yellow fan-shaped flowers. For dry positions. Frost tolerant. (V) **Plate 85**

GOODIA Family: Fabaceae

lotifolia 2 m
Common fast-growing shrub with blue-grey clover-like foliage and clustered yellow pea flowers with a dark patch on the standard. For semi-shade positions. Frost resistant. (N) **Plate 86**

GREVILLEA (Spider Flower) Family: Proteaceae

This family includes shrubs of prostrate habit through to tall trees, most of which are adaptable and long flowering. They are attractive to birds and the majority prefer a sunny position. Prune lightly after flowering.

Individual flowers are formed by a fusion of the petals or sepals to give a colourful perianth. In the young flowers this is tubular and encloses the stamens and pistil. As the flower matures, the perianth splits down one side, allowing the stigma to protrude (in a hook fashion). When the pollen is ripe the perianth splits into four, releasing the stigma which carries with it the pollen. This is subsequently removed by visiting birds or insects.

After the pollen has been removed from the stigma the perianth segments fall off, exposing the ovary, a swelling at the base of the style, and at this stage the stigma is receptive to pollen from another flower.

The fruit forms from the fertilised ovary as a tough follicle, with one or two seeds each with a winged margin.

The flowers may be arranged singly or in a cluster, giving the whole flower-head a 'spider-like' or 'toothbrush' appearance.

acanthifolia prostrate 1× 2 m
(Bear's Foot Grevillea). Dense, prickly, divided foliage and mauve-pink toothbrush flowers for long periods. Tolerates wet and frost conditions. (N)

alpina
(Alpine Grevillea). Very variable shrub found in many different forms, usually all long-flowering but variable in colour combinations of red through yellow.

***alpina* 'Grampians'** Prostrate to 2 m × 1 m
This form varies from prostrate to the form from Mt Zero which grows to approximately 2 m. All are noted for their spectacular orange and red flowers. **Plates 87, 88**

anethifolia 1.2 m
Very fine much divided foliage and cream flowers. Frost and drought hardy. (N) **Plate 89**

aquifolium Prostrate–2 m × 2 m
(Holly Grevillea). Many different forms available, most with prickly holly-like foliage, often greyish and hairy. Red toothbrush flowers in profusion, spring to summer. Requires moist position. Will tolerate considerable shade. (V) **Plate 90**

***aquifolium* 'Wartook'** Prostrate × 1.5 m
This form from Lake Wartook in the Grampians is very hardy and can be used for rockery planting.

arenaria 2 × 2 m
Oval greyish foliage and terminal red or yellow spider flowers (N)

Acacia adunca

2 *Acacia baileyana*

3 *Acacia beckleri*

cacia boormanni

5 *Acacia cardiophylla*

6 *Acacia cultriformis*

cacia decora

8 *Acacia decurrens*

9 *Acacia fimbriata*

cacia glaucescens

11 *Acacia howittii*

12 *Acacia iteaphylla*

13 *Acacia podalyriifolia*

14 *Acacia saligna*

15 *Actinotus helianthii*

16 *Alyogyne huegeli*

17 *Angophora hispida*

18 *Anigozanthos flavidus* 'Re

19 *Anigozanthos manglesii*

20 *Anigozanthos* 'Regal Claw'

21 *Banksia ericifolia* 'Burgundy'

22 *Banksia* 'Giant Candles'

23 *Banksia serrata*

24 Banksia spinulosa

Bauera capitata

26 *Bauera rubioides* 'White'

27 *Billardiera ringens*

Blandfordia nobilis

29 *Boronia denticulata*

30 *Boronia heterophylla*

Boronia megastigma

32 *Boronia muelleri*

33 *Boronia mollis* 'Lorne Pride'

Boronia pilosa 'Rose Blossom'

35 *Boronia serrulata*

36 *Boronia* 'Sunset Serenade'

37 *Brachycome angustifolium*

38 *Brachycome pilliganensis*

39 *Brachysema lanceolatum*

40 *Callistemon* 'Burgundy'

41 *Callistemon* 'Candy Pink'

42 *Callistemon* 'Harkness'

43 *Callistemon citrinus* 'White'

44 *Callistemon* 'Dawson River'

45 *Callistemon* 'Captain Cook'

46 *Callistemon* 'Demesne Rowena'

47 *Callistemon* 'Kings Park Special'

48 *Callistemon* 'Little John

Callistemon 'Mauve Mist'

50 *Callistemon* 'Mt Oberon'

51 *Callistemon phoeniceus* 'Pink Ice'

Callistemon pinifolius 'Green'

53 *Callistemon viminalis* 'Prolific'

54 *Callistemon* 'Reeves Pink'

Callistemon salignus

56 *Callistemon* 'Violaceus'

57 *Callistemon* 'Western Glory'

Cassia odorata

59 *Ceratopetalum gummiferum*

60 *Chamaelaucium uncinatum*

61 *Chamaelaucium uncinatum* 'Purple Pride'

62 *Chamaelaucium uncinatum* 'University Red'

63 *Chamaelaucium uncinatum* 'White'

64 *Chorizema cordatum*

65 *Clematis aristata*

66 *Correa* 'Dusky Bells'

67 *Correa* 'Marian's Marvel'

68 *Crowea exalata* × *saligna*

69 *Dampiera diversifolia*

70 *Dampiera trigona*

71 *Darwinia citriodora*

72 *Darwinia grandiflora*

Darwinia homoranthoides

74 *Elaeocarpus reticulatus* 'Pink'

75 *Epacris impressa* 'Bega form'

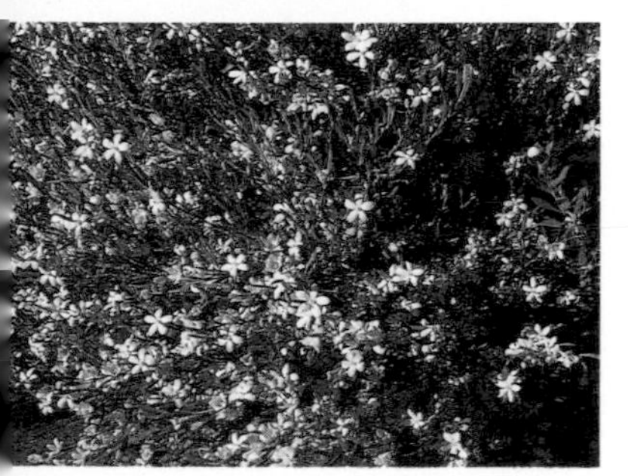

Eriostemon australasius

77 *Eriostemon myoporoides*

78 *Eriostemon nodiflorus*

Eucalyptus elata

80 *Eucalyptus forrestiana*

81 *Eucalyptus haemastoma*

Eucalyptus sideroxylon 'Rosea'

83 *Eucalyptus leucoxylon* 'Rosea'

84 *Eugenia wilsoni*

85 *Goodenia lanata*

86 *Goodia lotifolia*

87 *Grevillea alpina* 'Mt Zero fo

88 *Grevillea alpina* 'Grampians'

89 *Grevillea anethifolia*

90 *Grevillea aquifolium*

91 *Grevillea aspleniifolia*

92 *Grevillea banksii*

93 *Grevillea baueri*

94 *Grevillea biternata*

95 *Grevillea* 'Boongala Spinebill'

96 *Grevillea brachystylis*

Grevillea 'Canberra Gem'

98 *Grevillea* 'Clearview David'

99 *Grevillea* 'Coochin Hills'

Grevillea 'Dargan Hill'

101 *Grevillea dielsiana*

102 *Grevillea hookerana*

Grevillea jenkinsii

104 *Grevillea* 'John Evans'

105 *Grevillea juniperina*

Grevillea lanigera 'Mt Tamboretha'

107 *Grevillea lavandulacea* 'Victor Harbour'

108 *Grevillea longistyla*

109 *Grevillea* 'Misty Pink'

110 *Grevillea muelleri*

111 *Grevillea* 'Poorinda Constance'

112 *Grevillea* 'Poorinda Elegance'

113 *Callistemon* 'Candy Pink'

114 *Grevillea* 'Poorinda Rachel'

115 *Grevillea* 'Poorinda Royal Mantle'

116 *Grevillea* 'Poorinda Tranquility'

117 *Grevillea quercifolia*

118 *Grevillea* 'Robyn Gordon'

119 *Grevillea sericea* 'Collaroy Plateau'

120 *Grevillea* 'Shirley Howie'

Grevillea 'Sid Cadwell'

122 *Grevillea speciosa*

123 *Grevillea synapheae*

Grevillea triloba

125 *Hakea sericea* 'Pink'

126 *Hardenbergia comptoniana*

Hardenbergia violacea
'Happy Wanderer'

128 *Helichrysum baxteri*

129 *Helichrysum* 'Dargan Hill Monarch'

Hibbertia dentata

131 *Hibbertia empetrifolia*

132 *Hibbertia obtusifolia*

133 *Hibbertia scandens*

134 *Hibbertia serpyllifolia*

135 *Hibbertia vestita*

136 *Hibiscus heterophyllus* 'Lutea'

137 *Isopogon anemonifolius*

138 *Isotoma axillaris*

139 *Kennedia coccinea*

140 *Kennedia nigricans*

141 *Keraudrenia integri*

142 *Kunzea ambigua* 'Pink'

143 *Kunzea baxteri*

144 *Kunzea parvifolia* 'Dwarf'

Lambertia formosa

146 *Lechenaultia biloba*

147 *Lechenaultia formosa* 'Orange'

Lechenaultia formosa 'Sunrise'

149 *Leptospermum flavescens* prostrate

150 *Leptospermum scoparium* var. *rotundifolium* 'Jervis Bay'

Melaleuca armillaris

152 *Melaleuca erubescens*

153 *Melaleuca fulgens* 'Salmon'

Melaleuca incana

155 *Melaleuca lateritia*

156 *Melaleuca linariifolia*

157 *Melaleuca nesophila*

158 *Melaleuca quinquinervia*

159 *Melaleuca steedmanni*

160 *Melaleuca thymifolia*

161 *Melaleuca wilsonii*

162 *Micromyrtus ciliata*

163 *Myoporum floribundum*

164 *Myoporum parvifolium purpurea*

165 *Pandorea* 'Golden Show

166 *Pandorea* 'Snow Bells'

167 *Passiflora aurantia*

168 *Phyla nodiflorus*

Pimelia 'Bon Petite'

170 *Pimelia linifolia*

171 *Prostanthera denticulata*

Prostanthera 'Poorinda Ballerina'

173 *Prostanthera rotundifolia*

174 *Prostanthera saxicola* var. *montana*

Pultenaea capitallata

176 *Pultenaea villosa*

177 *Ricinocarpus pinifolius*

Rulingea hermanniifolia

179 *Scaevola albida* 'White'

180 *Scaevola humilis*

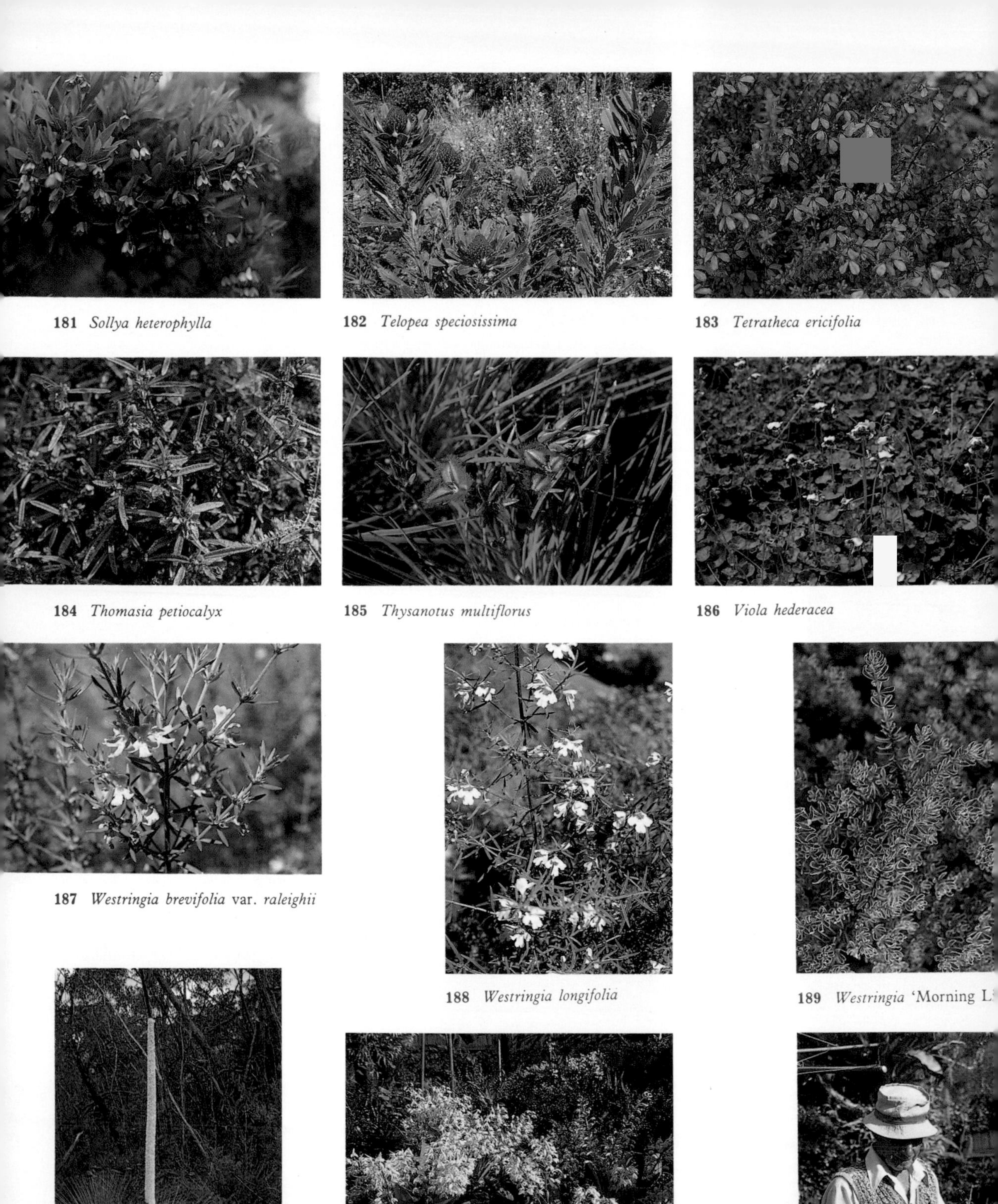

181 *Sollya heterophylla*

182 *Telopea speciosissima*

183 *Tetratheca ericifolia*

184 *Thomasia petiocalyx*

185 *Thysanotus multiflorus*

186 *Viola hederacea*

187 *Westringia brevifolia* var. *raleighii*

188 *Westringia longifolia*

189 *Westringia* 'Morning L

190 *Xanthorrhoea australis*

191 *Dendrobium* species

192 *Dendrobium kingianum* (right)

aspleniifolia 2–3 m × 2.5 m
Slender, upright shrub with long, stiff blue leaves and mauve toothbrush clusters, mostly in spring, but at other times. Frost resistant. (N) **Plate 91**

'Audrey' 3 m × 2.5 m
(*juniperina* × *rosmarinifolia*). Narrow oval pointed foliage and orange-red wheel flowers in winter and spring mostly.

'Austraflora Canterbury Gold' prostrate × 2 m
Glossy dark green foliage and pale gold flowers during winter and spring. Ideal large ground cover.

australis prostrate × 1 m
Good ground cover form with fine-scented flowers. Frost hardy. (N)

banksii 3 m × 2 m
Large shrub with much divided foliage and huge red flowers. For sunny, well-drained position. Requires pruning. (Q) **Plate 92**

***banksii* White** 3 m × 2 m
As above, with large cream flowers. (Q)

barklyana 2–7 m × 3 m
Large, irregularly lobed foliage and pale pink toothbrush flowers from late spring to summer. Suitable for clay soils and moist conditions. (N)

baueri 1.2 m
Closely packed oval foliage with rusty tips and deep red spider flowers. Will tolerate some moisture. Frost resistant. Several forms are found in cultivation. (N) **Plate 93**

bipinnatifida 50 cm × 2 m
(Grape Grevillea). Harsh, deeply serrated light green foliage and huge red toothbrush cluster. For hot, well-drained positions, some moisture. (W)

biternata prostrate 1 × 4 m
Mat of finely divided light green foliage and heads of creamy flowers from winter to spring. For open, well-drained position with some moisture. (W) **Plate 94**

'Boongala Spinebill' 1.2 × 2 m
(Possibly *bipinnatifida* × *caleyi*). Deeply serrated foliage, rusty at tips and red, quite large, toothbrush flowers. **Plate 95**

brachystachya 50 cm × 2 m
Attractive cascading shrub with fine foliage and pink flowers from spring to winter. (N)

brachystylis 50 cm × 50 cm
Small shrub with narrow hairy leaves. Dazzling red hairy flowers, mainly in spring. (W) **Plate 96**

brevicuspis 1 × 1.5 m
Stiff bronze-green, deeply divided and pointed foliage with attractive fine, scented white flowers in spring. (W)

brownii 1 m × 60 cm
Open, spreading shrub with red flowers from winter to spring. (W)

buxifolia 1–2 m × 2 m
(Grey Spider Flower). Crowded, stalkless oval leaves, brown at tips and grey woolly spider flowers most of year. For well-drained and coastal positions. Frost resistant. (N)

caleyi 2–3 × 3 m
(Caley's Grevillea). Soft grey-green divided foliage, pink tipped and hairy. Maroon toothbrush flowers most of year. For deep, well-drained moist soils. (N)

'Canberra Dwarf' 60 cm × 1 m
Low growing compact shrub with fine needle foliage and red spider flowers during winter and spring.

'Canberra Gem' 1–2 × 2 m
Dark green needle foliage and pink-red spider flowers winter to spring. Hardy, and frost resistant. **Plate 97**

capitellata 60 cm × 1 m
Low growing variable shrub with burgundy flowers in late winter. Useful rockery plant. (N)

chrysophaea 1.2–2.4 m
(Golden Grevillea). Rounded foliage with edges turned down, yellow flower-heads most of year, mainly winter to spring. For moist, protected position. (V)

'Clearview David' 2 m × 2 m
(Crosbie Morrison × *rosmarinifolia*). Dark green needle foliage and deep red spider clusters hanging from branches spring to summer. (V) **Plate 98**

'Clearview John' 1 m × 1 m
Blue-green foliage and yellow flowers. (V)

'Clearview Robin' 2 m × 2 m
Blue-green needle foliage and brilliant red-pink spider flowers hanging late winter to spring. (V)

confertifolia prostrate–1 × 3 m
Dense spreading shrub with needle-like foliage and mauve-red flowers. Hardy. (V)

'Coochin Hills' 5 m × 3 m
Small tree with divided foliage, large golden/yellow cone flowers for most of the year. Suitable for most well-drained positions. (Q) **Plate 99**

crithmifolia 1–2 × 1 m
Fine needle foliage and showy white flowers from pink buds. (W)

'Crosbie Morrison' 1–1.5 m × 2 m
(*lavandulacea* × *lanigera*). Attractive bushy shrub with dark green foliage and orange to red spider flowers winter to spring. Hardy.

dallachiana 50 cm–1 m
Compact shrub with thin needle foliage and red and ivory spider flowers in spring and winter. For part shade, cool and moist positions. Hardy. (N)

'Dargan Hill' 1 m × 1 m
Compact shrub with needle foliage and red wheel flowers for most of the year. **Plate 100**

dielsiana 2 m × 1 m
(Varnish Grevillea). Fine, prickly greenish-yellow varnished foliage and pink and yellow flowers in spring. For well-drained soil. Prune constantly. Also red form. (W) **Plate 101**

diminuta 30 cm × 3 cm
Broad oval foliage and clusters of rusty spider clusters. Frost resistant. (N)

dimorpha 1–2 m × 2 m
Three leaf-forms found (fine, medium, broad) and large, loose, brilliant red flowerheads in spring. Frost resistant. (V)

endlicheriana 2–3 m × 2 m
Upright habit and soft, fine greyish foliage with small pinkish-white fringed clusters on long branches most of year. Well-drained position. Frost resistant. (W)

ericifolia 30 cm × 1 m
Soft, needle-like foliage and red or pink flowers. Suitable for rockeries. (N)

evansiana 2 m × 2 m
Oval-shaped foliage and terminal burgundy hanging flowers. (N)

fasciculata 1 m × 2 m
Low, cascading shrub with narrow foliage and orange to scarlet flowers autumn to spring (W)

floribunda 1.7 m
Longish leaves with margins turned under, stems reddish, flowers red and felted. For warm position. (N)

X *gaudichaudii* Prostrate × 2 m
Naturally occurring hybrid between *G. laurifolia* and *G. acanthifolia*, lobed foliage, rusty at tips and burgundy toothbrush flowers from spring to summer. Frost resistant. (N)

glabrata 2–3 m × 2 m
Tall, bushy shrub with grey-green fan-shaped foliage and small lacy white flowers most of year. Requires some moisture. (W)

hookerana 2–3 × 3 m
(Toothbrush Grevillea). Handsome shrub with wiry foliage and brilliant red toothbrush clusters, mostly in spring for long periods. May be clipped. Useful as hedge. Frost resistant. (W) **Plate 102**

intricata 1–2 × 2 m
Intricate twisting long fine needles and cream flowers in spring. For semi-shade positions. (W)

'Ivanhoe' 2–3 × 3 m
(*aspleniifolia* × *caleyi*). Foliage deeply serrated, rusty at tips. Red toothbrush flowers in spring.

'Jenkinsii' 1–1.5 m
Attractive small-growing shrub with woolly needle leaves and red flowers. Hardy. **Plate 103**

jephcottii 1–3 × 2 m
Oval greyish foliage, densely packed on stems. Flowers cream-green terminal. Must be pruned. (V)

'Jervis Bay' form 2 m × 2 m
Oval, dark green foliage and deep pink toothbrush flowers. Excellent hedging variety. (N)

'John Evans' 1 m × 1 m
(*baueri* × *rosmarinifolia*). Hardy compact shrub with dark green foliage and masses of red-and-cream spider flowers in winter and spring. **Plate 104**

johnsonii 2–4 m
Long fine needle foliage and red spider clusters in spring. Hardy.

juniperina 1–2 m × 2 m
Hardy shrub with dark green needle foliage and red spider flowers in winter and spring. (N)

***juniperina* 'Prostrate Red'** 50 cm × 2 m
Hardy spreading shrub with needle foliage and red flowers in winter and spring. (N)

***juniperina* 'Prostrate Yellow'** 50 cm × 2 m
Ideal, spreading ground cover with light green needle foliage and yellow flowers during winter and spring. (N) **Plate 105**

***lanigera* 'Dwarf'** 60 cm × 1 m
Low growing hardy shrub with soft grey foliage and pink and cream flowers in winter and spring. (N)

***lanigera* 'Mt Tamboretha'** prostrate × 1.5 m
As for above but ground-hugging. **Plate 106**

laurifolia prostrate × 3 m
Large oval bronze-tipped foliage with prominent veins. Dark red toothbrush flowers. Requires some moisture. Frost resistant. (N)

lavandulacea 50 cm × 1 m
Small shrub with short, narrow blue-grey foliage, spectacular red and white flowers during winter and spring. Some of the better forms are 'Penola', 'Black Range', 'Billy Wing' and 'Victor Harbour' (green foliage). **Plate 107**

linearifolia 2 m
(Narrow-leaf Grevillea). Fine long foliage and weeping

open habit with mauve-pink flowers many times a year. Frost resistant. (N)

longifolia 2–3 × 3 m
Long serrated foliage and burgundy toothbrush flowers in spring. Prune after flowering. Frost resistant. (N)

longistyla 3–4 × 3 m
Tall-growing shrub with fine long leaves and red terminal flowers. Requires sheltered, moist, but well-drained position. (Q) **Plate 108**

'Magic Lantern' 75 cm × 1 m
(*crithmifolia* × *thelemanniana glauca*). Attractive small shrub with soft grey-green foliage and pretty red spider clusters hanging like lanterns from foliage in spring. Hardy.

miquelliana 2–3 m × 2.5 m
Dense shrub with oval foliage and masses of red terminal spider flower clusters summer to winter. Broad, fine and medium fine forms. (N)

'Misty Pink' 2–3 m × 2 m
Tall shrub with silvery-green much-divided leaves and large erect pink brush heads throughout the year. (Q) **Plate 109**

'Molonglo Hybrid' prostrate × 2 m
Vigorous low growing plant with short dark green needle foliage and apricot flowers in winter and spring. (N)

muelleri 50 cm × 50 cm
Low-growing shrub suitable for rockery planting with fine foliage and yellow terminal flowers in spring. (W) **Plate 110**

'Ned Kelly' 2 m × 2 m
(Mason's Hybrid). Similar in size and habit to *G.* 'Robyn Gordon' but flower colour is orange-red.

nudiflora 1× 2 m
Narrow foliage with scarlet flowers on runners from spring to summer. (W)

obtusifolia Prostrate × 2 m
Excellent groundcover with light green bushy foliage and red spider flowers in spring. Hardy and lush. (W)

oleoides 2 m × 1.5 m
Tall growing shrub with dark green lanceolate leaves and axillary clusters of red flowers in winter and spring. (N)

'Olympic Flame' 1 m
(*rosmarinifolia* × *dallachiana*). Sharp, short needle foliage and large drooping clusters of red flowers in summer. Dense.

parviflora 1 × 1 m
(Small-flowered Grevillea). Delicate small-growing shrub with needle foliage and soft pinkish flowers summer to autumn. Good rockery specimen. (N)

patentiloba 1 m × 1 m
Dense shrub with finely divided foliage and red toothbrush flowers in spring. (W)

pilulifera 1 m
Open shrub with hairy needle-like leaves and small woolly flowers with orange-red styles in abundant dense heads. Suitable for sandy soils. (W)

pinaster 1 m × 3 m
Bushy shrub with woolly branches and spreading, rather loose, one-sided flower-heads. prefers moist, clay soils. (W)

'Pink Lady' 50 cm × 1.5 m
Hardy, low growing plant with needle foliage and pink spider flowers in winter and spring.

'Pink Pearl' 1–2 × 2 m
Dense shrub with deep green needle foliage and bright pink flowers from winter through to spring. Suitable for hedge planting. Frost resistant.

'Pink Pixie' 1 m × 1 m
(*rosmarinifolia* form). Spectacular pink flowering plant with masses of spider-like flowers during winter and early in spring. Very hardy.

polybractea 1–2 m × 2 m
Woolly long foliage and orange-red dense hanging clusters from spring to winter. (N)

'Poorinda Beauty' 1 m × 1 m
(NSW *juniperina* × *alpina*). Needle foliage and tight clusters of orange-red flowers winter to summer.

'Poorinda Blondie' 2 m
(*hookerana* seedling). Yellow toothbrush flowers and much-divided foliage.

'Poorinda Constance' 2.5 × 2.5 m
(NSW *juniperina* × *victoriae*). Soft linear foliage and red wheel flowers continuously. **Plate 111**

'Poorinda Diadem' 2.5–3 m
('Poorinda Leane' seedling). Oval leaves in fan-like arrangement surround yellow and buff wheel flowers in spring.

'Poorinda Elegance' 2.5 × 2.5 m
(NSW *juniperina* × *alpina/obtusifolia*). Twisted fine linear to oval foliage. Yellow and red wheel flowers most of year. **Plate 112**

'Poorinda Firebird' 2 × 2 m
(*speciosa* × *oleoides*). Profuse fiery red flowers on old wood from winter to summer. Good hedge plant.

'Poorinda Golden Lyre' 1 × 1 m
(*alpina* × *victoriae*). Blue-green oval leaves and golden-yellow claw flowers.

'Poorinda Hula' 1 × 2 m
(*trinervis* × *linearis*). Light arching habit and fine mauve spider flowers late spring and summer.

'Poorinda Illumina' 1 × 1 m
(*lavandulaceae* × *lanigera*). Short fine blue-green foliage and brilliant red flowers hanging from branches in spring.

'Poorinda Leane' 2.5 × 2.5 m
(NSW *juniperina* × *victoriae*). Dense shrub, soft linear foliage and orange wheel flowers almost continuously **Plate 113**

'Poorinda Marion' 1 × 1 m
(*dallachiana* × 'Poorinda Ruby'). Needle leaves, hanging red flower clusters several times a year.

'Poorinda Peter' 2–3 × 2 m
(*acanthifolia* × *aspleniifolia*). Serrated leaves deeply bronzed. Deep red toothbrush flowers spring to summer. Requires regular pruning.

'Poorinda Pink Coral' 1 × 2 m
(NSW *juniperina* × *victoriae*). Yellow-green foliage and pink spider flowers.

'Poorinda Queen' to 2 m × 2.5 m
(NSW *juniperina* × *victoriae*). Soft needle-like foliage and pink to orange spider clusters many times a year.

'Poorinda Rachel' 1 m × 2 m
(*alpina* × *juniperina*). Heavy oval foliage and large but tight orange-red wheel clusters in summer. **Plate 114**

'Poorinda Rondeau' 1 m × 3 m
(*lavandulacea* × *baueri*). Dark green needle-like leaves and red flowers up stems late winter to spring.

'Poorinda Rosy Morn' 1 m
As for *G.* 'Poorinda Rondeau', but improved.

'Poorinda Royal Mantle' Prostrate × 4 m
(*laurifolia* × *willisii*). Excellent vigorous dense groundcover plant with irregularly shaped leaves and red toothbrush flowers held above foliage mat. **Plate 115**

'Poorinda Signet' 1.5 m × 1.5 m
(NSW *juniperina* × *lanigera*). Curled oval leaves, silvery below. Cream and salmon-pink wheel clusters in spring.

'Poorinda Stephen' 1.2 m
(*oleoides* × *speciosa*). Narrow oval leaves, silvery below. Huge spider clusters of dark red flowers in summer.

'Poorinda Tranquillity' 1 m × 1.5 m
(*lavandulacea* × *alpina*). Attractive light green oval foliage and pastel pink flower clusters in summer. **Plate 116**

quercifolia 70 cm × 1 m
Small shrub with serrated foliage and mauve/purple erect flower heads during spring. (W) **Plate 117**

repens prostrate × 2 m
(Creeping Grevillea). Low, spreading grevillea with dark green holly-like foliage and dark red and green toothbrush flowers. Requires well-drained position with some moisture, semi-shade. (V)

rivularis 2.5 × 2.5
(Carrington Falls Grevillea). Much divided prickly green and bronze foliage with blue-mauve toothbrush flowers. (N)

robusta 20–30 cm
(Silky Oak). Tall, elegant, quick-growing tree with divided feathery foliage, bronze-tipped when young. Orange toothbrush flowers in summer. (N)

'Robyn Gordon' 1 × 2 m
(*bipinnatifida* × *banksii*). Large, deeply serrated foliage and huge orange-red double-sided toothbrush flowers all year. (Q) **Plate 118**

rogersii 1 m × 1.2 m
Shrub with narrow habit. Small, sparse foliage and red flowers in spring. (SA)

rosmarinifolia 2–3 × 2 m
(Rosemary Grevillea). Dark green needle foliage. Red and cream flowers from spring. Hardy, fast growing, frost tolerant. (N)

'Sandra Gordon' 3–4 m × 2 m
Medium to tall shrub with long divided foliage and spectacular large golden toothbrush flowers mainly in late winter and early spring. Heavy pruning required to keep plant compact. (Q)

'Scarlet Sprite' 1.5 m × 1 m
Small compact shrub with needle foliage and scarlet spider flowers for long periods in spring and sometimes in autumn. Hardy.

sericea 1–2 m × 2 m
With pruning, a dense shrub with narrow oval foliage and delicate pink flowers most of the year. For well-drained position and coastal planting. Frost resistant. White form also available. (N) **Plate 119**

shiresii 3–4 m × 4 m
Graceful, quick-growing shrub with large oval foliage with red veins. Flowers borne inside shrub are slightly bluish in colour, but insignificant.

'Shirley Howie' 1.5 m × 1.5 m
(*capitellata* × *sericea*). Small, reliable shrub with dense glossy foliage and mauve-pink flowers for long periods in spring. **Plate 120**

'Sid Cadwell' to 2 m × 2 m
Variable shrub with divided foliage and bright red toothbrush flowers for most of year. **Plate 121**

singuliflora prostrate–30 cm × 1 m
Low-growing and spreading shrub with green oval leaves, wavy margined. Single green flowers. (Q)

speciosa 2–3 m × 2 m
(Red Spider Flower). Bushy shrub with dark green stalkless foliage and loose deep red spider clusters at tips of shoots all year. Quick growing, takes pruning. (N) **Plate 122**

stenomera 2 m × 1 m
(Lace Net Grevillea). Long, narrow, slightly greyish foliage and red waxy flowers in loose terminal wheels most of year. (W)

synapheae prostrate × 1 m
Variable leaves taper to stalk and are usually three-lobed Flowers in 'catkin' clusters, cream. (W) **Plate 123**

thelemanniana prostrate × 3 m
(Spider Net Grevillea). Much divided foliage and scarlet flowers with yellow-tipped styles. Green leaf form most adaptable, but glaucous (grey-leaf) form prefers sun and tolerates coastal soils and frost. Requires sub-surface moisture. (W)

triloba 2.5 m × 2.5 m
Coarse grey-green triple foliage and highly perfumed cream flowers in leaf axils. Quick growing and hardy. Keep pruned. (W) **Plate 124**

tripartita 3–5 × 3 m
Erect-growing shrub with sharp, short grey-green foliage and single scarlet and orange flowers in winter. (W)

vestita 2 m × 3 m
(Rusty Grevillea). Wedge-shaped, three-forked foliage with masses of white (or mauve and white) flowers in upper leaf axils in spring. (W)

victoriae 2–3 × 2 m
(Royal Grevillea). Several leaf forms found, from longish oval to short oval, all with large red flowers in winter. Frost resistant. (N)

'White Wings' 2–2.5 m × 3 m
Very fast growing with masses of fine white flowers in winter and spring. Hardy.

GUICHENOTIA Family: Sterculiaceae

macrantha 60 cm–1 m × 1 m
Pale grey fine leaves and purple bell-shaped flowers winter to spring. Well-drained position. (W)

HAKEA Family: Proteaceae

Shrubs and trees with tough, alternate leaves, many differing shapes and sizes. The flowers are closely related to those of *Grevillea*, but differently arranged. The seed pods are woody and split into two to release two winged seeds. Most prefer sunny, well-drained position, but quite hardy.

bakerana 3 × 2 m
Dense bush with long needle leaves and pink spidery flowers in profusion. Very hardy. (N)

dactyloides 2–2.5 m
Bushy shrub with narrow leaves and masses of small cream flowers in tangled clusters. (N)

elliptica 3 m × 2.5 m
Erect, bushy shrub with dense crown. New growth bronze, and white flowers clustered around stems in spring. (W)

eriantha 2 m × 2.5 m
Leaves narrow and pale green, silver-grey buds open to white or pinkish flowers in clusters. Hardy. (N)

laurina 4 m × 2.5 m
(Pincushion Hakea). Narrow oval leaves with longitudinal veins. Flowers arranged as red and cream 'pincushion' clusters in autumn. For protected position and coastal. Frost resistant, but unsuited to humid coastal conditions. (W)

multilineata 3 m × 3 m
(Grass-leaf Hakea). Very long, fine foliage and white and scarlet flower spikes. Suited to hot positions, but difficult. Frost resistant. (SA, W)

petiolaris 3 × 3 m
(Sea Urchin Hakea). Grey oval foliage, silver when young. Flowers dull purple, 'pincushion' clusters in autumn. For light soils but also coastal positions. Frost resistant. (W)

purpurea 1 m × 1.5 m
Fine, divided and sharp-pointed foliage with showy spikes of crimson flowers along its branches in spring. Frost resistant. (N, Q)

salicifolia 4 × 4 m
(Willow-leafed Hakea). Useful, fast-growing and bushy shrub which acts as an excellent screen. Foliage is oval and light green with bronzed tips. White flowers in dense clusters in spring. Suitable also for coastal planting. Frost resistant. (N)

***salicifolia* 'Fine Leaf'**
Similar to above but foliage is very long and narrow.

sericea 2.5 m × 2 m
(Silky Hakea). Upright bush with sharp, long needle leaves and flowers along main stems for long period. White and pink and weeping forms found. Frost resistant. (N) **Plate 125**

suaveolens 3 × 3 m
(Sweet-scented Hakea). Sharply pointed and divided

foliage, broad when young. Flowers white and scented in spring. Suitable for coastal planting and all but wet positions. Frost resistant. (W)

teretifolia 2 m
(Dagger Hakea). Long, sharply-pointed foliage and creamy white nectar-filled flowers in summer and spring. Frost resistant. (N)

HARDENBERGIA Family: Fabaceae

comptoniana Groundcover or Climber
(Native Wisteria). Usually ground-hugging and spreading with leaves in groups of three and a profusion of showy sprays of blue-purple flowers in spring. For sunny, well-drained and dry positions. (W) **Plate 126**

violacea
(False Sarsaparilla). Single large leaves and sprays of intense purple flowers in spring. Form varies from climbing to bushy or prostrate. White and pink flowering forms also available. (N)

***violacea* 'Happy Wanderer'**
An improved form showing more vigour, larger flowers. **Plate 127**

HELICHRYSUM Family: Asteraceae

Usually groundcover or border plants with paper-like flowers which last for months when picked.

apiculatum 30 cm × 1.5 m
(Common Everlasting). Dense spreading shrub with silver-grey hairy foliage and clusters of small, deep yellow flower-heads from spring to autumn. For sunny, well-drained position. Prune hard in spring. (N)

baxterii 20 cm × 30 cm
(White Everlasting). Narrow foliage, silky below, clump habit. Snow-white daisies from spring to summer. For sunny rockeries. (N) **Plate 128**

bracteatum 50 cm × 1 m
(Golden Everlasting). Lance-shaped woolly leaves. Large golden flowers spring and summer. (N)

'Dargan Hill Monarch' 50 cm × 1 m
Large woolly green leaves with huge golden paper daisies all year. Hardy. Sunny, open positions. (Q) **Plate 129**

'Diamond Head' 20 cm × 60 cm
Small compact herbacous plant with soft and slightly hairy foliage. Flowers are yellow-gold and papery, held above foliage during summer. (N)

ramosissima prostrate × 1 m
Low-growing, spreading plant with soft grey foliage and small gold flowers for most of the year.

HELIPTERUM (Paper Daisy) Family: Asteraceae

albicans 20 cm × 30 cm
This species varies considerably and has several forms. Tall, thin flower stems are hairy, with creamy daisy-like flowers in summer.

HEMIANDRA Family: Labiatae

pungens prostrate × 1 m
(Snake Bush). Small, rigid, pointed foliage and flowers which are mauve-pink with red spots in spring and summer. For open, well-drained, sunny position. Also upright and white forms. (W)

HIBBERTIA (Guinea Flower) Family: Dilleniaceae

dentata prostrate × 50 cm
Attractive trailing shrub with almost bronze foliage in winter months and bright yellow flowers from winter for long periods. (N) **Plate 130**

empetrifolia prostrate × 1 m
Small, coarse foliage and bright yellow flowers in spring for long periods. Excellent ground cover. (N) **Plate 131**

microphylla 50 cm × 50 cm
Small rockery plant, tiny leaves along stems and bright yellow open flowers during spring and summer. (N)

obtusifolia prostrate × 1 m
Cascading small plant with oval fleshy leaves and bright yellow flowers. Requires some moisture. (N) **Plate 132**

pedunculata 20 cm × 60 cm
Semi-prostrate plant tending to root at nodes and carrying yellow open-petalled flowers in spring. (N)

procumbens prostrate × 1 m
Dense mat of fine green foliage and gold flowers in abundance most of year. (N)

scandens climber or prostrate
(Snake Vine). Twining or trailing shrub with large glossy leaves and huge yellow buttercup flowers from spring to summer. For open, sandy soils and coastal spots. (N) **Plate 133**

sericea 30 cm × 60 cm
Small shrub with small leaves and yellow silky flowers in spring.

serpyllifolia prostrate × 1 m
Small foliage, varnished in texture, and huge open-petalled yellow flowers throughout the year. Suitable for well-drained positions. (N) **Plate 134**

stellaris 20 cm × 60 cm
Fine small shrub with orange buttercup flowers from spring to autumn. Appreciates moist position. Suitable tub plant. (W)

vestita prostrate × 60 cm
Compact plant with very small leaves and large yellow flowers. **Plate 135**

HIBISCUS Family: Malvaceae

heterophyllus 3 m × 3 m
Long green foliage and large white flowers with purple centre. For sunny, dry position. Also yellow form. (N) **Plate 136**

tileaceus 3–5 m × 3.5 m
Coastal shrub with roundish, heart-shaped leaves, white and hairy beneath. Large yellow flowers summer to autumn. (N)

HOMORANTHUS Family: Myrtaceae

darwinioides 1 m
Small, thin greyish leaves and pendulous pink, yellow and green flowers in spring. For sun or semi-shade. Frost resistant. (N)

flavescens 1 × 1.2 m
Fine short, light grey-green foliage on symmetrical and spreading branches. Small pale pink and white flowers. For dry position. (N)

virgatus 1.2 m × 1.2 m
Erect small shrub with small yellow flowers. For dry sandy soils. (N)

HOYA Family: Asclepiadaceae

australis
(Australian Wax Plant). Climber with thick shiny leaves and clusters of waxy white flowers. (N)

HYMENOSPORUM Family: Pittosporaceae

flavum 9 × 4.5 m
(Native Frangipanni). Attractive tree with greyish bark and shiny green leaves. Cream or yellow scented flowers in spring. Hardy. (Syd)

HYPOCALYMMA Family: Myrtaceae

angustifolium 1 × 1 m
(Native Peach Blossom). Long fine foliage and deep pink and cream fluffy flowers all down branches from late winter to spring. Protect from wind. Frost resistant. (W)

cordifolium 1 × 1 m
Compact, hardy small shrub with heart-shaped leaves on red stems and numerous small white flowers. Suitable for semi-shade. Frost resistant. (W)

***cordifolium* 'Variegated'** 60 cm × 60 cm
Compact shrub with strong yellow variegation. Tiny white flowers in spring. Hardy and frost tolerant.

robustum 1 × 1 m
Glorious shrub with narrow leaves and rich pink flowers, gold tipped in spring. Difficult, requiring warm, sandy, well-drained soils. Cool, open position. Frost resistant. (W)

INDIGOFERA Family: Fabaceae

australis 2.5 × 1 m
Fern-like foliage with young growth blackish on surface. Sprays mauve pea flowers in spring. Very hardy and frost resistant. Suitable for semi-shade, poor dry soils. Prune after flowering. (N)

ISOPOGON (Cone Bush) Family: Proteaceae

anemonifolius 1.8 m × 1.2 m
Divided foliage and almost globular cones opening to yellow flowers in spring. Frost resistant. (N) **Plate 137**

anethifolius 2 m × 1.2 m
Foliage finer than *I. anemonifolius* and cones ovoid. Flowers yellow in spring. Very hardy and frost resistant. (N)

dawsoni 1 m × 1 m
(Nepean Conebush). Hardy shrub, suitable for most soils and positions. Yellow cone-like flowers in spring. (N)

ISOTOMA Family: Lobeliaceae

axillaris
(Rock Isotome). Low bushy perennial with ragged leaves. Long-stalked bright blue tubular star flowers. (N) **Plate 138**

fluviatalis
(Swamp Isotome). Creeping mat of rooting stems. Soft blue star flowers. (N)

JACKSONIA Family: Fabaceae

scoparia 5 m × 2.5 m
(Dogwood). Small tree of weeping habit with soft light orange pea flowers. For open sunny position. Frost and snow tolerant. (N)

JASMINUM Family: Oleaceae

suavissimum light climber
Semi-shrub like plant with twining branches and lanceolate leaves. Fragrant cream flowers in spring and summer. (N)

KENNEDIA Family: Fabaceae

coccinea
(Coral Vine). Vigorous twining or trailing plant requiring plenty of room. Oval bronze foliage and showy orange to red pea flowers. (W) **Plate 139**

eximia
Excellent ground cover with small maroon flowers for long periods from winter to spring. Open positions. (W)

glabrata
Usually completely prostrate with small leaves and pleasantly perfumed mauve-scarlet flowers held on short stems. Good leafy cover for sun or filtered sun, requires some moisture. (W)

microphylla
Small prostrate species with tiny oval leaves and small dark brown-red flowers on short stems. (W)

nigricans
(Black Bean). Extremely vigorous twiner or ground cover with large leaves and huge black-purple flowers with yellow blotch on standard. Bud attractive. May be kept under control in dry shady spot. (W) **Plate 140**

prorepens
Prostrate shrub for sunny conditions with some available moisture. Purplish flowers (Central Aust.).

prostrata
(Running Postman). Creeper with attractive wavy margined oval leaves and brilliant red flowers winter to summer. For well drained sunny spot. (N)

rubicunda
(Dusty Coral Pea). Extremely vigorous plant with large leaves and red flowers. Can be used as climber or ground cover but needs to be controlled.For coastal situations. (N)

stirlingii
Vigorous plant with light green foliage and orange-red pea flowers spring and summer. (W)

KERAUDRENIA Family: Sterculiaceae

integrifolia 60 cm × 1 m
Hardy plant with greenish-brown hairy foliage and blue flowers during spring and summer. Suitable for most positions including semi-shade. **Plate 114**

KUNZEA (Tick Bush) Family: Myrtaceae

ambigua 2 × 2.5 m
Tall shrub with narrow leaves and showy white flowers packed at ends of branches. Must be pruned. Very hardy. Pink form also available. (Syd) **Plate 142**

'Badja Carpet' prostrate × 2 m
Prostrate plant with small obovate leaves and spreading, reddish stems which tend to root at nodes. Flowers are white and fluffy and appear in summer. (N)

baxteri 2 × 2.5 m
Attractive oval foliage and large crimson and gold-tipped bottlebrush flowers on terminal shoots in spring and summer. Hardy, but needs well-drained position. (W) **Plate 143**

capitata 1.5 × 1.5 m
(Pink Buttons). Narrow, short foliage and deep pink knobby heads in spring. Very hardy. (N)

parvifolia 50 cm × 1.5 cm
Small spreading bush with tiny leaves and small violet flowers in tight clusters in spring. Moist soils preferred. (N) **Plate 144**

pomifera 50 cm × 4 m
Creeping plant for sandy soils with attractive cream-coloured brushes followed by edible berries. (V)

pulchella 1.8 m × 2 m
Dense shrub with crowded greyish silky foliage and rich red short bottlebrush flowers in spring and summer. For sunny, well-drained position. (W)

recurva 2 × 2 m
Large shrub with fine leaves tapered to stalk and spreading outwards on stems. Rosy lilac flowers in dense rounded heads in spring. Hardy, tolerating periods of wetness. (W)

LAGUNARIA Family: Malvaceae

patersonia 10 × 4 m
(Norfolk Island Hibiscus). Tree with oval foliage suitable for providing shade. Large pink bell flowers in autumn. Hardy, suitable for coastal planting. (N)

LAMBERTIA Family: Proteaceae

formosa 2 m × 2.5 m
(Honey Flower). Dense bush with narrow, tapering leaves, pointed at ends. Red tubular spiked flowers all year. Suitable for sun or shade, provided well-drained. Fruits known as 'Mountain Devils' for their shape. (N) **Plate 145**

LECHENAULTIA Family: Goodeniaceae

All from Western Australia, these small plants are usually not easy to grow in Sydney. Require well-drained (built up) flower beds with winter moisture. All flower for most of year. Mostly prostrate to 50 cm. Treat as annuals.

biloba
Soft blue-green needle leaves and brilliant blue flowers. **Plate 146**

formosa
Many forms and cultivars found. Flowers brilliant reds and yellows and combinations of these colours.

***formosa* 'Orange'**
Soft green needle leaves on suckering stems and masses of orange flowers mainly in spring and summer. **Plate 147**

***formosa* 'Prostrate Red'**
Superb dark red flowers on bright green carpeting foliage.

***formosa* 'Sunrise'**
Green upright foliage and brilliant orange flowers with haloes of red, borne throughout the year but in profusion during spring. Excellent pot specimen. **Plate 148**

LEPTOSPERMUM (Tea Tree) Family: Myrtaceae

Shrubs and small trees with aromatic leaves and open flowers with waxy centres. Excellent for hedge planting and low windbreaks. Many species are suitable for poorly-drained soils. All are hardy.

'Cardwell' 2 m × 2 m
(*flavescens* form). Dense shrub with weeping branches and white open-petalled flowers in spring. New foliage has attractive red stems.

'Copper Glow' 3 m × 2 m
(*petersonii* form). Tall-growing weeping shrub with copper-coloured foliage and white open-petalled flowers in spring.

flavescens 3 × 3 m
(Common Tea-tree). Fine greenish-red foliage and white flowers. Suitable also for coastal planting. Frost resistant. (N)

flavescens prostrate 60 cm × 1.5 m
(syn. 'Pacific Beauty'). Low spreading shrub with fine foliage on pendulous branches and masses of open-petalled white flowers during spring. Hardy. **Plate 149**

juniperinum 30 cm × 1 m
Spreading, somewhat stiff shrub with pointed foliage and masses of white flowers in spring. Frost resistant. (N)

laevigatum 3 m × 3 m
(Coast Tea-tree). Large shrub with oval leaves and grey stringy bark. White flowers in summer. Salt and frost resistant. (N)

lanigerum 3 × 3 m
(Woolly Tea-tree). Greyish-coloured leaves and weeping habit, masses of white flowers late spring. Hardy, takes moist position. Frost resistant. (V)

petersonii 5 m
Fine, attractive lemon-scented foliage, reddish when new. White flowers in spring and summer. Quick growing and suited to coastal planting. (N)

scoparium* var. *rotundifolium
Dense shrub with rounded leaves and large white or pale pink flowers in spring. Frost resistant. (N) **Plate 150**

squarrosum 1.5 m × 2 m
(Peach Blossom Tea-tree). Bushy, erect shrub with small pointed leaves and huge single flowers on old wood from late summer to autumn. Very hardy. Frost resistant. (N)

LIVISTONA Family: Arecaceae

australis to 25 m
(Cabbage Tree Palm). Tall tree with slender stem and fan-like foliage. Makes an excellent indoor specimen. (N)

LOMANDRA Family: Xanthorrhoeaceae

longifolia 60 cm × 1 m
Large tussock-like plant with narrow strap-like leaves. Crowded flower spikes on flattened stems. Suitable for rockery planting and for most soils and positions. (N)

LOMATIA Family: Proteaceae

silaifolia 50 cm × 1 m
(Wild Parsley). Much divided foliage and many cream flowers held in spikes above bush in summer. (N)

MAZUS Family: Scrophulariaceae

pumilio
(Swamp Mazus). Rosette with solitary mauve flowers on short stalks, spreads easily in moist situations.

MELALEUCA (Paperbark) Family: Myrtaceae

This genus comprises prostrate shrubs to small trees, the majority of which prefer moist conditions. The flowers are in spikes with numerous conspicuous stamens which give the whole the appearance of a 'bottlebrush'. The flowering head is usually much smaller than that of the *Callistemons*.

armillaris 5 m
(Bracelet Honey Myrtle). Fast-growing bushy tree with fine green foliage and white brushes in spring. Hardy, salt tolerant and suitable for any soil conditions. (N) **Plate 151**

***armillaris* 'Pink'**
As above but with pink flower brushes.

***bracteata* 'Gold'** 4–5 m
Upright bushy tree with yellow-gold foliage. Flowers insignificant. Grown mostly for outstanding foliage colour contrast. Frost tender.

***bracteata* 'Golden Gem'** 1 m
Low-growing shrub with variegated yellow-green foliage and small cream brushes in summer.

***bracteata* 'Revolution Green'** 5–7 m
Upright bushy small tree with bright green foliage and profuse white brushes in summer. May be trimmed.

calothamnoides 2–3 m × 1 m
Rounded small bush with soft greyish needles and pale red brushes from spring to summer. Hardy. (W)

conothamnoides 1–2 m × 2 m
Open bush requiring well-drained position. Terminal heads of red flowers September to November. Suits sandy soils. (W)

decussata 3–4 m × 2.5 m
(Cross-leaf Honey Myrtle). Dense shrub with tiny foliage and short mauve brushes in spring. Coastal positions also. Frost resistant. (N)

diosmifolia 4 m × 2 m
Compact, salt tolerant shrub with stiff leaves and greenish-yellow brushes. Extremely hardy. (W)

elliptica 2.5 m × 2.5 m
(Granite Honey Myrtle). Blue-grey rounded foliage and large red brushes in summer. Open, well-drained positions and coastal. Frost resistant. (W)

ericifolia 3–5 × 3 m
(Swamp Paperbark). Adult foliage fine and green, pale yellow brushes in late spring. Suitable for over-wet soils. Frost resistant. (W)

erubescens 3 m × 1.2 m
Compact, fine green foliage, pink to mauve brushes in summer. Suitable for moist soils. (N) **Plate 152**

***fulgens* 'Purple'** 3 m × 2 m
Tall, open shrub with narrow foliage and spectacular purple bottlebrush flowers, mainly during summer. Hardy. (W)

***fulgens* 'Salmon'** 3 m × 2 m
Tall, open shrub with salmon-pink bottlebrush flowers for long period during late winter and spring. Hardy. (W) **Plate 153**

huegelii 2–3 × 3 m
(Chenille Honey Myrtle). Small foliage and white terminal brushes. Suitable for seaside planting. (W)

hypericifolia 3 × 2.5 m
(Red Honey Myrtle). Arching habit and pretty oval leaves. Deep orange-red brushes in late spring and summer. Suitable for open and coastal planting. (N)

incana 2–2.5 m × 2.5 m
(Grey Honey Myrtle). Beautiful weeping greyish foliage and pale yellow brushes in profusion in spring. Requires light soil and open position. Good specimen tree. Frost resistant. (N) **Plate 154**

lateritia 2 m × 2 m
(Robin-Redbreast Bush). Sparse low-growing shrub with deep orange to red brushes continuously from winter. Suitable for medium to heavy soils with moisture. (W) **Plate 155**

linariifolia 5–7 m
(Snow-in-Summer). Fine leaves and white flowers in abundance late spring to summer. Frost tender, but salt tolerant. (W) **Plate 156**

micromera 1–2 m × 1 m
Low spreading shrub with curiously scaly foliage and pyramidal habit. Compact yellow ball flowers in spring. Very hardy. Frost resistant. (W)

nesophila 2.5 m × 3 m
(Lavender Paperbark). Attractive small tree with oval foliage and pink terminal brushes in summer. For open, well-drained and coastal positions. (W) **Plate 157**

nodosa 2–3 m × 1–3 m
Large to medium bush with fine foliage and cream but gold-tipped flower balls in spring. (N)

pulchella 50 cm × 1.2 m
(Claw Flower). Short foliage and claw-shaped mauve flowers early in summer. Frost resistant. (W)

quinquenervia 10 m
(Broadleaf Paperbark). Handsome tree with dense head and cream brushes in summer. Suitable for coastal planting. (N) **Plate 158**

radula 3–3.5 m
Narrow foliaged, open shrub with mauve bottlebrush flowers. Hardy. (W)

radula × fulgens 3 m
Foliage wider than parent, mauve bottlebrush flowers, gold-tipped, several times a year. Hardy. (N)

spathulata 1–1.5 m
Wide-spreading shrub with tapered foliage and pink to red flowers in small heads spring to summer. Hardy. (W)

squamea 2–3 m × 2 m
Oval pointed or narrow leaves with creamy-purple flowers in dense heads at tops of stems in spring. (N)

squarrosa 4 m
(Scented Paperbark). Dense small shrub with stiff dark green foliage and strongly-scented cream brushes. Can be pruned. (N)

***steedmanni* 'Red'** 1–2 × 1.5 m
Pleasing greyish foliage and large scarlet brushes, yellow tipped in spring. Light to medium soil and open position. Frost resistant. (W) **Plate 159**

***steedmanni* 'Purple'**
As above but with purple brushes in spring. (W)

styphelioides 5–8 m
(Prickly Paperbark). Large, dense-growing small tree with prickly foliage and dense creamy brushes in summer. Frost resistant. (N)

thymifolia 1 m × 1 m
(Thyme Honey Myrtle). Small-growing shrub with fine leaves and deep mauve fringed flowers early spring. (N) **Plate 160**

violacea prostrate × 1 m
Low-growing, spreading shrub with small heart-shaped leaves and violet flower clusters in spring. Frost resistant. (W)

wilsonii 2 m × 2 m
(Crimson Honey Myrtle). Sharp pointed leaves and red to pink brushes in profusion in spring. For open position and also coast. (V) **Plate 161**

MELIA Family: Meliaceae

azedarach 10 m
(White Cedar). One of few native deciduous trees with doubly compound leaves and lilac blossoms in spring. Very hardy, suitable for open, moist position. Frost resistant. (N)

MICROMYRTUS Family: Myrtaceae

ciliata 70 cm × 70 cm
Tiny dense shrub with crowded dark green leaves and very small white flowers in spring. Suitable for rockery planting. For sunny and well-drained positions. Frost resistant. (N) **Plate 162**

MICROSTROBOS Family: Podocarpaceae

fitzgeraldii prostrate–1 m
Straggling shrub with drooping green branchlets and tiny

spirally arranged leaves. Cone bearing. Found only at Wentworth Falls in reach of spray.

MILLETIA Family: Fabaceae

megasperma
(Native Wistaria). Vigorous climber with large dark green glossy leaves and masses of purple flowers in spring. Prefers partial shade. Frost tender. (N)

MIRBELIA Family: Fabaceae

dilatata 2 m × 2 m
Neat shrub with wedge-shaped foliage, somewhat wavy and pointed. Mauve pea flowers among upper leaves in spring. For sunny and dry positions. Hardy. (W)

oxylobioides 3 m × 2 m
Attractive shrub with small foliage and orange and red pea flowers in spring. Hardy in well-drained position. Frost resistant. (V)

MUEHLENBECKIA Family: Polygonaceae

axillaris
(Australian Ivy). Rampant ground cover or climber with small dark green shield-shaped foliage. On weldmesh a hedge-like effect. Waxy flowers somewhat insignificant. Frost resistant. (N)

MYOPORUM Family: Myoporaceae

debile prostrate × 1 m
(Amulla). Long, narrow blue-green leaves and pink star flowers, followed by cream and purple berries. Suitable for open, dry position. (N)

floribundum 2.5 m × 3 m
(Slender Boobialla). Small tree with narrow, long, drooping, somewhat sticky foliage and tiny white flowers clustered among its branches in spring. For sunny, well-drained position. Frost resistant. (N) **Plate 163**

parvifolium prostrate × 1 m
(Creeping Boobialla). Fleshy foliage and white star flowers. Excellent mat plant with widespread rooting. Fine, medium and broad leaf, also purple-stemmed forms available. For sunny, well-drained positions with some moisture, for best results. Frost resistant. (N) **Plate 164**

viscosum 3 × 3 m
(Sticky Boobialla). Fine oval foliage which surrounds the white, hairy flowers. Young growth sticky. Hardy, dense shrub. (V)

OLEARIA (Daisy Bush) Family: Compositae

erubescens 1 m
Shrub with narrow leaves, somewhat woolly beneath. White daisy flowers in clusters. (N)

floribunda 1 m × 1.2 m
Small, neat shrub with tiny leaves and white daisies in leafy sprays. (N)

iodochroa 1 m × 1 m
Small-growing shrub with violet daisies in flat clusters. Suited best to semi-shade conditions. (N)

phlogopappa 1.5 m × 2 m
(Otway Daisy Bush). Upright-growing slender bush with woolly leaves and white, blue or pink daisy flowers from spring to summer. Takes pruning. Prefers sheltered, moist position. Frost resistant. (N)

teretifolia 1.5 m
(Slender Daisy Bush). Dense bush with tiny leaves packed closely to stems. Pale-blue or white daisies in flat-topped clusters. For any moist position. (N)

OREOCALLIS Family: Proteaceae

wickhami 7–10 m
(Tree Waratah). Beautiful tree for sheltered warm coastal situations with narrow long stalked leaves and large flat topped red Waratah-type flower clusters. (N, Q)

ORTHROSANTHUS Family: Iridaceae

multiflorus 50 cm
(Morning Flag). Hardy shrub with grass-like leaves and blue flowers on tall stems in spring. (SA)

PANDOREA Family: Bignoniaceae

'Golden Showers'
(*pandorana* form). Tall, woody climber with fine divided

leaves and gold and brown bell-flowers in grape-like clusters during spring. (N) **Plate 165**

jasminoides
(Bower Plant). Tall, showy climber with bushy compound leaves and sprays of large white purple-throated flowers for long periods from summer. (N)

pandorana
(Wonga Vine). Tall, woody, twining plant with compound leaves and small velvety tubular flowers, usually white and pink throats in spring. (N)

'Snow Bells'
(*pandorana* form). Vigorous climber with masses of small cream bell flowers in grape-like clusters during spring. Hardy. (N) **Plate 166**

'Snow Queen'
(*jasminoides* form). Beautiful lush climber with dark green glossy foliage and large contrasting white bell flowers for long periods from summer on. Hardy. (Q)

PASSIFLORA Family: Passifloraceae

aurantia
Glorious tendril climber with large glossy lobed foliage and large flowers, red in bud and opening red and white. Superb fence cover for year-round colour. **Plate 167**

cinnabarina
(Red Passion Flower). Vigorous climber with attractive dark green lobed leaves and dark red flowers late in spring. For sheltered position, but frost resistant. (N)

PATERSONIA Family: Iridaceae

Perennials with erect, grass-like leaves and flowers which are a succession of short-lived blue or purple heads on long stalks lasting for many months. All prefer open, moist positions, preferably clays.

glabrata
Light purple flowers in spring. (N)

longiscapa
(Native Flag). Pale green leaves, purple flowers, late spring and summer. (V)

sericea
(Native Iris). Dark leaves and purple flowers. (N)

PELARGONIUM Family: Geraniaceae

australe 50 cm × 50 cm
Rounded shrub with oval fleshy leaves and flowers usually white but purple veined. (N)

rodneyanum 15 cm × 30 cm
(Magenta Storks Bill). Neat little ground-hugging plant with leaves in rosette and reddish-purple flowers in summer. Open, dry position. (V)

PERSOONIA (Geebung) Family: Proteaceae

nutans 1 m × 1 m
(Nodding Geebung). Small to medium sized shrub with short fine leaves and yellow flower clusters on short stalks like lanterns summer to autumn. (N)

oxycoccoides prostrate × 1 m
Prostrate form with small oval leaves slightly bronzed when new. Masses of tiny yellow flowers within mat from spring to summer. (N)

pinifolius 2 m × 2 m
Graceful pine-leaved shrub with beautiful spikes of yellow flowers at branch ends in summer. (N)

PETROPHILE Family: Proteaceae

sessilis 2 m × 1.2 m
(Drumsticks). Rigid, much-divided, foliage and yellow to white cone flowers in summer. For sunny, well-drained position. (N)

PHEBALIUM Family: Rutaceae

dentatum 2 m
Attractive shrub with clustered yellow flowers along branches. (N)

squamulosum 1 m × 1.2 m
Narrow silver foliage and rich golden terminal flowers in spring. For well-drained, reasonably moist soils. (N)

PHILOTHECA Family: Rutaceae

salsolifolia 1 m × 30 cm
Heath-like shrub with crowded narrow leaves and pale mauve star flowers in spring. Sheltered, well-drained position. (N)

PHYLA Family: Verbenaceae

nodiflora prostrate × 2 m
Lawn plant for dry areas. Mat-type foliage and clusters of pink flowers in summer. Frost resistant. (N) **Plate 168**

PIMELEA (Rice Flower)
Family: Thymelaceae

'Bon Petite' 1 m × 1 m
Small shrub with oval shiny leaves and very deep pink pom-pom flower heads for long periods from spring. Hardy. Suitable for coast positions. **Plate 169**

ferruginea 1 × 1 m
(Pink Rice Flower). Dome-shaped shrub with glossy small oval leaves and masses of pink terminal flowers in spring. For sunny, well-drained position, any soils, and also coastal planting. (W)

ligustrina 1.5 M
(Tall Rice Flower). Bushy shrub with soft light green foliage and large white pin-cushion flowers in droopy clusters. (N)

linifolia 1 m × 60 cm
Narrow, small leaves and white flowers, tinged pink all year. Frost resistant. (N) **Plate 170**

PITTOSPORUM
Family: Pittosporaceae

phillyreoides 4–6 × 2 m
(Weeping Pittosporum). Slender tree with drooping branches and willowy leaves. Yellow flowers in spring, followed by yellow fruits. For warm, dry position. Frost resistant. (N)

revolutum 3.5 × 2.5 m
(Brisbane Laurel). Shrub to small tree, with hairy undersurface to foliage and yellow bell flowers in spring. Large yellow fruit. Frost resistant. (N)

rhombifolium 8 × 4.5 m
(Queensland Pittosporum). Erect tree with shining deep green leaves and creamy fragrant flowers in spring, followed by small yellow berries. Suitable for protected position. Frost resistant. (Q)

undulatum 5 × 3 m
(Native Daphne). Bushy tree with light green leaves and creamy fragrant flowers in spring. Suitable for shaded position. (N)

PLATYTHECA
Family: Tremandraceae

verticillata 50 cm × 50 cm
Small erect, heath-like plant with whorls of linear leaves and masses of dark blue nodding flowers in spring and summer.

PLECTRANTHUS
Family: Lamiaceae

parviflorus Prostrate × 3 m
Vigorous herbaceous plant with felt-like aromatic foliage and spikes of light blue flowers in spring and summer.

POA
Family: Gramineae

australis
Grassy clump with blue-green leaves. Very hardy. Frost tolerant. (N)

PODOCARPUS
Family: Podocarpaceae

lawrencei prostrate — 1.5 × 1 m
(Mountain Plum Pine). Small gnarled, semi-prostrate conifer with broad leaves and deep red round succulent fruits. For cool position. Slow growing. (N)

spinulosus to 2 m
Bushy spreading shrub to small tree with purplish-black fruits. (N)

PRATIA
Family: Lobeliaceae

pedunculata
Mat plant for cool moist positions with blue or white star flowers in summer for long periods. (N)

PROSTANTHERA (Mint Bush)
Family: Labiatae

This family comprises more than 70 species, all of which are Australian. The foliage is usually aromatic and the flowers tubular with two lips, the upper of which is two-lobed and often hooded, and the lower of which is three-lobed and spreading. Most require moist, semi-shade positions.

aspalathoides 30 cm × 1 m
(Scarlet Mint Bush). Clusters of tiny needles and orange to red flowers in spring for long periods. Requires sandy sheltered position. (N)

baxteri* var. *sericea 2 m × 1 m
Bushy, erect shrub with greyish foliage and blue flowers in spring. Hardy in well-drained position. Withstands dry conditions. (N)

calycina 50 cm × 1 m
Low bushy shrub with round hairy leaves and orange to red flowers in spring. Lime tolerant and suitable for coastal planting. (SA)

cryptandroides 75 cm × 1 m
Small shrub with small slender leaves and lilac to mauve flowers for most of the year. Hardy, suitable for most positions. (N)

cuneata 1 m × 1.2 m
(Alpine Mint Bush). Round, shiny foliage and large white flowers tinged with purple in spring and early summer. Frost resistant. (N)

denticulata prostrate × 1 m
(Rough Mint Bush). Low-growing and spreading shrub with slightly rough foliage and mauve flowers in profusion in spring. For sun or part shade, some moisture. (N) **Plate 171**

incana 1 m × 1.5 m
(Hoary Mint Bush). Small, broad, rough, greyish, hairy leaves and large violet-blue flowers crowded at branch ends in spring. Suitable for coastal planting also.

incisa 1–2 m × 1.5 m
Broad-toothed leaves and small, broad-lobed lilac flowers. Showy. (N)

lasianthos 3–5 m × 2.5 m
(Victorian Christmas Bush). Tall shrub with large-toothed and pointed leaves and big white flowers around Christmas. Fast growing. (V)

melissifolia 3 m × 2 m
Tall shrub with oval, toothed leaves and lilac flowers in long open sprays at ends of shoots, early in summer. Very hardy. Also pink form. (V)

nivea 2–3 × 2 m
(Snowy Mint Bush). Slender, smooth needle leaves, slightly grey in colour, with large white or blue flowers late in spring. (N)

ovalifolia 2–3 × 2 m
Many forms of this fast-growing bush, usually with narrow oval leaves pointed at the ends. Mauve flowers in short end sprays in spring. Long-lived provided not over-watered. (N)

phylicifolia 1.5 m × 1 m
Shiny green foliage and fragrant purple flowers with yellow or violet throat. (N)

'Poorinda Ballerina' 2 m
(*phylicifolia* × *lasianthos*). Attractive shrub with white flowers tinged lilac covering bush in spring. Hardy. **Plate 172**

'Ragged Robin' 3 m
(*staurophyla X ovalifolia*). Foliage very ragged and blue flowers in leaf axils, spring.

rhombea 1 × 3 m
Shrub with small, rounded leaves and pale blue-mauve flowers covering bush in spring. Compact habit. (N)

rotundifolia 1.5 m × 1.2 m
(Round-leaf Mint Bush). Adaptable shrub with lilac end sprays in spring. Frost resistant. (V) **Plate 173**

saxicola* var. *montana 20 cm × 1.5 m
Low-growing, but spreading, mint bush with pale mauve flowers. Extremely hardy. (v) **Plate 174**

sieberi 1 m × 1.5 m
Tall, slender shrub with broad-lobed toothed leaves and violet flowers in spring. (N)

stricta 1.8 × 1.8 m
Compact shrub with bright green foliage and small purple flowers in spring. Adaptable. (W)

violacea 1 × 1 m
Small, bushy shrub with violet flowers in spring. (N)

walteri 1 m × 1.5 m
(Alpine Mint Bush). Coarse dark green foliage and unusual smoky-grey flowers for long periods spring to summer. Very hardy, suitable in heavy soils in full sun. (N)

PULTENAEA (Bush Pea)
Family: Fabaceae

capitellata prostrate × 1 m
Bushy shrub with small grey foliage and golden-yellow pea flowers summer to autumn. (N) **Plate 175**

cunninghamii prostrate × 2 m
Most attractive groundcover plant with diamond-shaped foliage, sometimes reddish. Brown and yellow flowers at leaf bases in spring and summer. For well drained positions. (N)

daphnoides 1–2 m × 2 m
Wedge-shaped leaves with rounded ends and small point. Showy clusters of yellow pea flowers at ends of leafy branches in spring. (N)

flexilis 2–3 × 2 m
(Yellow Bush Pea). Pale green oval foliage and bright yellow flowers covering bush in spring. For moist, semi-shaded positions. (N)

villosa 1.5 m × 1.5 m
Soft leafy shrub with sprays of yellow flowers. For well-drained positions. (N) **Plate 176**

REGELIA Family: Myrtaceae

ciliata 1.5 m × 1 m
Erect shrub with small oval foliage and mauve flowers in dense round cushions from spring to summer. For sunny, dry position. (W)

RESTIO Family: Restionaceae

tetraphyllus 1 m
Creeping rhizomatous plant with erect stems, often over 1 m high, with finely divided bright green branchlets giving a plume-like effect.

RHAGODIA (Saltbush) Family: Chenopodiaceae

nutans prostrate × 30 cm
(Nodding Saltbush). Vigorous groundcover with light green triangular foliage and red berries. Suitable for heavy soils. (N)

spinescens 60 cm × 2 m
Dense low bushy cover with greyish triangular foliage. Very hardy and salt tolerant. (N)

RHODODENDRON Family: Ericaceae

lochae 80 cm × 80 cm
Low spreading shrub with ovate dark green thick textured leaves. Brilliant red trumpet flowers in clusters, spring and summer. Ideal indoor or tub specimen plant.

RICINOCARPUS Family: Euphorbiaceae

pinifolius 1.5 m × 1 m
(Wedding Bush). Erect shrub with soft needle leaves and large white star flowers in fragrant small clusters covering bush in spring. Suitable for well-drained sandy soils in sun. (N) **Plate 177**

RULINGIA Family: Sterculiaceae

hermanniifolia prostrate × 2 m
Dense groundcover shrub with attractive rough crinkled foliage and masses of small heads of pink and white flowers in spring and summer. Most adaptable and salt resistant. (Syd) **Plate 178**

SCAEVOLA (Fan Flower) Family: Goodeniaceae

aemula prostrate × 1 m
(Fairy Fan Flower). Sprawling plant, but dense. Oval bright green leaves and deep mauve flowers from spring to summer. Suitable for cut flowers. Excellent rockery plant for cool, moist position. Frost resistant. (N)

albida prostrate 50 cm × 1 m
Suckering groundcover plant with pale mauve flowers. For moist position. (Syd) **Plate 179**

calendulacea prostrate × 2 m
(Dune Fan Flower). Excellent vigorous coastal sand-binder with thick leaves and sky blue flowers. (N)

humilis prostrate × 30 cm
Low-growing plant with oval, fleshy leaves and masses of small purple flowers in summer. (N) **Plate 180**

SCHEFFLERA Family: Araliaceae

actinophylla 6 m
(Umbrella Tree). Beautiful tree with large round compound leaves, umbrella-like at tops of stems. Honey-laden red flowers packed aong 1 m stalks spring to summer. Excellent indoor plant specimen. (Q)

SCLERANTHUS Family: Caryophyllaceae

biflorus × 60 cm
(Canberra Grass). Mossy carpeting plant with insignificant flowers. Suitable for rockeries. Frost tolerant. (N)

uniflorus
Mossy carpeting plant similar to above but finer in all detail. For cool positions. Frost tolerant. (N)

SOLLYA Family: Pittosporaceae

heterophylla climber
(WA Bluebell Climber). Bright green foliage and brilliant blue clustered bell flowers. Strongly twining. For sunny, well-drained position. Pink and white forms also available. Frost resistant. (W) **Plate 181**

SOWERBAEA Family: Liliaceae

juncea 30 cm × 30 cm
Spectacular tufted perennial with rosette of leaves at ground level. Brilliant mauve spring flowers in dense terminal clusters. Easy to grow, prefers moist conditions. Frost resistant. (N)

SPYRIDIUM Family: Rhamnaceae

cinereum prostrate × 1.2 m
Pretty trailer with attractive heart-shaped leaves and hairy flowers above spreading whitish floral leaves in summer. Coastal. (N)

obcordatum prostrate × 1 m
Small ground cover-type plant with very small round leaves and grey hairy flowers in spring.

STENOCARPUS Family: Proteaceae

sinuatus 6 m
(Firewheel Tree). Slow-growing tree with glossy dark green sinuate leaves and scarlet wheel-shaped flowers from summer to autumn. Frost tender when young. Prefers hot, moist, protected position. (N)

STYPANDRA Family: Liliaceae

caespitosa 30 cm × 50 cm
Small tufted plant with grass-like foliage and blue star flowers held on slender stems during spring. (N)

SWAINSONA Family: Fabaceae

galegifolia 1 m × 1.5 m
(Darling River Pea). Free-flowering sub-shrub with long sprays of red flowers all year. Prune back in winter. Suitable for any dry, sunny position. (N)

SYNCARPIA Family: Myrtaceae

glomulifera 10 × 5 m
(Turpentine). Upright, dense-foliaged tree with stringly fibrous bark and white flowers. Very hardy. (N)

SYZYGIUM Family: Myrtaceae

paniculatum 6 m × 4 m
Handsome and hardy tree with glossy leaves, rust-coloured when new. Large white fluffy flowers in spring followed by dark red berries. (Q)

TECOMANTHE Family: Bignoniaceae

hillii climber
Vigorous twining plant with dark green leaves and large reddish bell-shaped flowers in summer. Spectacular plant for semi-shade conditions. (Q)

TELOPEA Family: Proteaceae

speciosissima 3 m
(NSW Waratah). Erect shrub with tough leathery leaves and huge crimson flower-heads in spring. (N) **Plate 182**

TETRATHECA Family: Tremandraceae

ciliata 30 cm × 60 cm
(Pink Eye). Roundish leaves and bright purple-pink four-petalled flowers in spring. For well-drained, sandy soils, semi-shade. (SA, T, V)

ericifolia 30 cm × 60 cm
Narrow leaves in rings of four and red flowers on slender stalks spring to summer. Semi-shade positions and well-drained. Frost resistant. (N) **Plate 183**

THOMASIA Family: Sterculiaceae

petiocalyx 30–50 cm × 60 cm
(Paper Flower). Bushy shrub with woolly leaves and lilac-pink flowers hanging in loose clusters in spring. For well-drained position. Hardy. (V) **Plate 184**

purpurea 50 cm
Small bushy shrub. Large purple papery flowers. (W)

THRYPTOMENE Family: Myrtaceae

baeckeacea 50 cm × 1 m
Hardy small shrub with long cascading branches and masses of pinkish flowers in late winter for long periods. Suitable for warm, well-drained position. (W)

calycina 1 m × 2 m
(Bushy Heath Myrtle). Narrow-leaved shrub with small white flowers packed along stems in winter. Suitable as cut flowers. Prefers sandy soils. (V)

saxicola 1 m × 2 m
(Rock Thryptomene). Almost weeping in habit, this shrub has numerous oval overlapping leaves and small pale-pink stalked flowers from winter to spring. Frost resistant. (N)

***saxicola* 'F. C. Payne's Hybrid'** 1 × 3 m
Low-spreading bush with well-spaced tiny oval leaves and light pink but small flowers in profusion in winter for long periods. Suitable for cut flowers. Open, well-drained position preferred.

THYSANOTUS Family: Liliaceae

multiflorus 30 cm
Small, tufted plant with delicate lacy mauve three-petalled flowers for short periods in spectacular numbers during spring. Suitable for any but wet positions. (W) **Plate 185**

TOONA Family: Meliaceae

australis to 40 m
(Red Cedar). Large deciduous tree with huge trunk. Pinnate leaves and fragrant flowers in sprays at ends of branches in spring. (N)

TRISTANIA Family: Myrtaceae

conferta 9 m
(Brush Box). Attractive tree with rough lower trunk but smooth pink to red upper limbs. Broad leaves and white flowers. Excellent for shade. Suitable for open position. (N)

laurina 5 m
(Water Gum). Attractive small tree with glossy dark leaves and small yellow flowers in summer. For sheltered position, moist and coastal soils. May be cut back to produce large shrub 3–4 m. (N)

VIMINARIA Family: Fabaceae

juncea 4-5m × 2 m
(Native Broom). Small fast-growing tree for heavy or poor soils and boggy conditions. Yellow sprays in spring. Prune after flowering. (N)

VIOLA Family: Violaceae

hederacea
Creeping plant with ivy-like leaves and pale mauve flowers held on erect stems for long periods spring and summer. Excellent ground cover for moist positions. (N) **Plate 186**

WAHLENBERGIA (Australian Bluebell) Family: Campanulaceae

gloriosa
Mat creeper found in the highlands among rocks. Deep azure-purple flowers from summer to autumn. Tends to die back in winter. (N)

WESTRINGIA Family: Labiatae

brevifolia* var. *raleighii 2 m × 2 m
Tall bushy shrub with fine blue-grey foliage and blue flowers for long periods from spring. Particularly hardy and quick growing. Suitable most positions including coastal planting. (T) **Plate 187**

fruticosa 2 m × 1.5 m
(Coast Rosemary). Extremely hardy shrub with fleshy grey-green foliage and white flowers on and off the whole year. Suitable for exposed conditions, frost and coastal planting. May be pruned. (N)

glabra 1 m × 2 m
Bushy shrub with pretty oval foliage and delicate lilac flowers from spring to summer. For semi-shaded position. (N)

longifolia 2 m × 1 m
Attractive hardy shrub with long fine leaves and white flowers in abundance several times a year. Frost tolerant. (N) **Plate 188**

'Morning Light' 1 m × 1 m
(*fruticosa* form). Variegated dwarf shrub with cream/green foliage. Specially suitable for rockery or pot culture. Very hardy. **Plate 189**

XANTHORRHOEA Family: Xanthorrhoeaceae

australis
(Blackboy). Extremely slow-growing plant, normally available 'dug' under license. Ensure it has been in container for several months before transplanting to the ground. Very hardy, once established. Suitable for sunny well-drained positions. Brilliant specimen plant. (N) **Plate 190**

Orchids

Orchids are protected plants and it is illegal to remove them from the bush. Care should be taken that any clumps purchased bear the NPWS cloth licence tag.

Although there is a certain mystique attached to the growing of orchids, they are really quite easy to grow.

The beauty of orchids is unsurpassed in the flowering world and many of the Australian species are delicately perfumed. The varieties most commonly sold in the Nursery are those familiarly found growing on trees and shrubs as aerial-rooted plants (epiphytes) or on rocks (lithophytes). Probably the least demanding of all plants, in nature they exist mainly on decomposing particles of bark, leaf mould and bird or insect droppings. Some orchids grow in the soil (terrestrials) and certain of these are saprophytic, growing in association with decayed wood. Most of the temperate orchids are terrestrials and are usually only available from specialist orchid nurseries.

The flowers are quite different from those of other flowering plants. The petals and sepals are both coloured and the particular parts peculiarly adapted for their special methods of pollination.

Most species do well in the open or under trees, thriving on filtered sunlight. They are also suitable for partly shaded and not too windy balconies.

Dendrobium species are generally extremely adaptable, growing in sun or shade, potted in compost, or on rocks or trees. Quite large clumps fixed to comparatively small blocks of tree fern fibre will grow happily for many years and in this manner a great number of different species can be grown in a relatively small area. The number of leads or growths per plant may be increased by occasionally cutting the main stem between the last mature but still green pseudobulb and the completely dormant one behind it. In most instances a new growth will come from the base of the old pseudobulb. The growth fibre may be supplemented by watering with soluble plant food. **Plate 191**

Dendrobium aemulum
(White Feather Orchid). Variable species with highly scented slender white flowers carried on dozens of spikes in spring.

Dendrobium beckleri
Pendulous stems with upright leaves and delicate pale mauve flowers. Requires good light.

Dendrobium falcorostrum
(Beech Orchid). Sweetly scented orchid with long slender pseudobulbs or canes and short sprays of waxy white flowers. Suitable for pots, better tied to suitable host.

Dendrobium gracilicaule
Long slender canes and masses of sweetly scented flowers from pale to dark yellow with backs speckled brown.

Dendrobium kingianum
(Pink Rock Lily). Semi-epiphytic, requiring good light and water in growing season. Flowers vary in size and colour from pure white through pinks to deep red. **Plate 192**

Dendrobium linguiforme
(Tongue or Thumbnail Orchid). Quaint fleshy tongue-shaped leaves attached to rock surfaces. Dainty perfumed flowers in sprays of twenty or more snow-white blooms. Best attached tightly to rock or tea tree slab. Not suitable for pots.

Dendrobium speciosum
(Rock Lily). Most spectacular of native orchids. Fragrant golden flowers borne on large spikes. Form from Hawkesbury Sandstone is rock-dweller, that from the north coast tree-dweller with longer canes (var. *hillii*). May be grown on trees, cut stumps, rockeries, etc. Requires ample sunlight.

Dendrobium teretifolium
(Bridal Veil Orchid). Pencil-leaved orchid usually found on Casuarina. Thousands of sweetly scented flowers in spring. For light position.

Sarcochilus falcatus
(Orange Blossom Orchid). Dainty epiphyte which is easily grown in garden and suitable for shady position. Requires moist atmosphere and good light. Strongly perfumed flowers white or red, yellow or purple.

Thrixspermum tridentatum
(Tangle Orchid). Tiny orchid with powerful perfume. Roots grow in tangled masses hanging precariously from small twigs.

Ferns

All tree fern species, elkorn, staghorn and bird's nest ferns marked * are protected in NSW and should only be purchased if they bear a cloth licence tag issues by the NPWS.

Tree Ferns

***Cyathea australis**
(Rough Tree Fern). Slender fast-growing fern. Dull green fronds with butts persisting towards top or trunk. Tolerant of sun provided roots kept moist. Requires frost protection. Suitable for tub.

***Cyathea cooperi**
Quick-growing species. Fronds shed cleanly leaving neat scar. Tolerant of sun if base is sheltered. Base of fronds covered in short reddish-brown spines and larger white scales.

***Dicksonia antarctica**
(Soft Tree Fern). Slow-growing species. Thick trunk covered with reddish-brown hairs provides excellent host for epiphytic orchids and ferns. Long fronds always present horizontally. Easy but requires shaded position with plenty of water, applied preferably to crown and trunk. Tops may be sawn off and replanted but bottom will not continue to grow. Fronds may be cut off if damaged by heat or frost, reshooting quickly in warm months but more slowly in winter. Sticky clay subsoils unsuitable.

***Todea barbara**
(King Fern). Slow growing with short thick trunk and a number of crowns of fronds. Suitable for protected positions and tub planting.

Ground Ferns

Adiantum aethiopicum
(Common Maidenhair). Delicate looking fern for moist positions. Suckers profusely from underground rhizomes, fronds 15–30 cm tall with wiry stems. Also for pots. Requires ample sunlight.

Adiantum capillus-veneris
(Large-leaf Maidenhair). As above but fronds have larger pinnules.

Adiantum formosum
(Giant Maidenhair). Handsome vigorous species for tub or ground with large, much-branched fronds. Frost hardy.

Adiantum hispidulum
(Rough Maidenhair). As above but with white hairs on pinnules. Easy and hardy. For semi-protected position. Frost hardy.

Asplenium bulbiferum
(Mother Spleenwort). Finely divided fronds at ends of which are an abundance of small plantlets. These eventually take root and may then be transplanted. Suitable for pot or sheltered position in ground, excellent basket fern. Requires shelter from frost.

Asplenium flabellifolium
(Necklace Fern). Weakly trailing species which proliferates from tips of the fronds. Suitable for pot or basket, protected in ground or epiphytically on tree fern species.

***Asplenium australasicum**
(Bird's Nest Fern). Large epiphyte with long broad radiating fronds to collect debris as growing medium. Relatively small root system. Suitable for tub, basket or flower-box cultivation. Prefers dry, shaded spots. Frost tender.

Blechnum cartilagineum
(Fishbone Fern). Fronds arising from central clump with light green wavy pinnules. Hardy.

Blechnum nudum
(Fishbone Water Fern). Hardy, widespread species with thick erect rhizome which eventually grows to about 1 m.

Blechnum patersonii
(Strap Water Fern). Excellent species for wet shady positions. Frond shape very variable.

Culcita dubia
(False Bracken, Rainbow Fern). Hardy, brackenlike fern for shaded or exposed position. Tolerates considerable sun.

Cyclosorus truncatus
(Giant Creek Fern). Forms tall spreading tussock on thick fibrous trunk. Cool, moist spot.

Doodia aspera
(Prickly Rasp Fern). Widespread fern with harsh pinnate fronds, bright pink when young. Excellent rockery subject. Hardy in variety of situations.

Doodia cordata
(Small Rasp Fern). Very variable fern, narrow soft fronds. For pot or protected position.

Doodia media
(Common Rasp Fern). Hardy species with purple new fronds.

Gleichenia dicarpa
(Pouched Coral Fern, Tangle Fern). Forms large tangled thickets but also suitable for pot or tub culture provided roots wet and plenty of sun. Minute pinnules on slender wiry fronds.

Histiopteris incisa
(Batswing Fern). Useful filling fern with large upright soft fronds. For tub or open ground.

Lygodium japonicum
Unusual fronds palmately lobed. For sheltered position. Frost tender.

Marsilea drummondii
(Nardoo). Unusual species in which rhizome grows in wet, muddy situations bearing a number of erect fronds with clover-like pinnae which float when submerged. For shallow water tanks and boggy situations.

Nephrolepis cordifolia
(Fishbone Fern). Hardy for both indoor and outdoor, pots or open ground. Tolerates shade or sun.

Polystichum formosum
(Broad Shield Fern). Feathery fronds. Particularly hardy.

Polystichum proliferum
(Mother Shield Fern). Attractive soft feathery fern which proliferates from plantlets at frond ends. Frost hardy, suited to sunny or shaded positions.

Pteris tremula
(Tender Brake). Fast-growing, freely colonising species for a range of positions.

Pteris umbrosa
(Jungle Brake). Forms an attractive clump in protected open ground position or pot.

Pyrrosia rupestris
(Rock Felt Fern). Extensively creeping small fern found on rocks or trees. Small round fronds. For pot, basket or tied to branch.

Sticherus flabellatus
(St John Umbrella Fern). Tall erect fern with terminal fronds held like 'umbrellas'. Slow-growing. For damp position.

Elkhorns & Staghorns

Platyceriums are remarkably specialised ferns which form their own self-contained system. Nest leaves are spreading and form an efficient collecting device. These are replaced annually and the old leaves curl inwards to collect all the humus. The roots of the fern gradually grow into this humus. True fronds are thinner and pendulous, bearing spores in a mass of brownish sporangia. These fronds are produced only at intervals and fall off when old.

****Platycerium bifurcatum***
(Elkhorn). The commonest and most widespread species; found on trees, boulders or rock faces in a variety of habitats. True fronds branch in the upper half, being wedge-shaped at base. Nest leaves deeply lobed, green when new turning papery-brown with age. This fern may spread into huge clumps which are easily divided. Tie onto smooth barked tree or fix onto a board, preferably with sphagnum moss and peat in equal parts wedged between. Requires overhead shelter in frost areas. Likes strong but not direct sunlight and needs its peaty base kept moist with at least a daily soaking in summer. Excellent in basket culture.

****Platycerium superbum***
(Staghorn). Possibly the most spectacular fern, getting larger each year. Nest leaves always green and true fronds of larger specimens may dangle over 2 m. Young specimens may take several years to produce true leaves. May be mounted on piece of tree or tied to board. Must be protected from wind and direct sun and kept moist. Frost tender. Do not water in winter in cold areas.

Fern Ally

Selaginella uliginosa
(Swamp Selaginella). Mat species forming carpet of mossy foliage. Suitable for pot culture or as ground cover in moist conditions.

Plant Lists

The plant lists have been compiled from many different sources, some of which have proved contradictory. Since we also no longer know the source of our parent plants, it must be stressed that the lists are but well-intentioned recommendations of plants worth trying in a particular location. Readers' help in improving these lists would be much appreciated.

For Frost Areas

Those plants listed in ***bold type*** are considered to be frost resistant, the others are suitable for mild frosts only and may suffer some damage in heavy frosts.

Acacia ***baileyana***, ***beckleri***, ***boormanni***, ***brownii***, ***buxifolia***, *cardiophylla*, *cultriformis*, *dealbata*, ***decora***, ***decurrens***, *drummondii*, *elata*, ***fimbriata***, *howittii*, *linifolia*, ***longifolia***, ***mearnsii***, ***melanoxylon***, *podalyriifolia*, *pycnantha*, *pravissima*, *prominens*, *rotundifolia*, *rubida*, ***spectabilis***, ***suaveolens***, ***vestita***
Acmena smithii
Angophora costata
Anigozanthos ***flavidus***, spp.
Astartea fascicularis
Baeckea virgata
Banksia ***asplenifolia***, ***collina***, integrifolia ***marginata***, *robur*, ***serrata***, *spinulosa*, *ericifolia*
Bauera ***rubioides***, ***sessiliflora***
Billardiera spp.
Blandfordia nobilis
Boronia ***anemonifolia***, ***deanei***, ***denticulata***, *heterophylla*, ***megastigma***, ***mollis***, ***molloyae***, ***pinnata***, *serrulata*
Brachychiton acerifolium, *populneum*
Brachycome multifida
Brachysema lanceolatum
Bulbine bulbosa
Callistemon ***brachyandrus***, ***citrinus***, ***pallidus***, ***phoeniceus***, ***pinifolius***, ***salignus***, ***sieberi***, ***viminalis***
Callitris ***rhomboidea***
Calytrix ***sullivanii***, ***tetragona***
Calocephalus brownii
Calothamnus ***gilesii***, ***quadrifidus***, ***villosus***
Cassia artemisioides, *nemophila*
Casuarina ***cunninghamiana***, *torulosa*, *nana*, *stricta*
Ceratopetalum gummiferum
Chorizema cordatum
Cissus antarctica
Clematis aristata, *microphylla*
Conostylis aculeata, *stylidioides*
Correa ***alba***, ***backhousiana***, *baeuerlenii*, *decumbens*, 'Mannii', *pulchella*, *reflexa*
Crowea exalata × *saligna*, *saligna*
Cryptandra amara
Dampiera diversifolia, *stricta*
Darwinia citriodora, ***fascicularis***, ***homoranthoides***
Dianella ***revoluta***, ***tasmanica***
Diplarrena ***moraea***
Dodonaea ***viscosa***
Eleocarpus ***reticulatus***
Epacris ***impressa***, *longiflora*, ***pulchella***
Eremophila ***glabra***, ***maculata***
Eriostemon ***myoporoides***
Eucalyptus ***blakelyi***, *botryoides*, ***camaldulensis***, *caesia*, ***calophylla*** **'Rosea'**, ***cinerea***, ***curtisii***, ***elata***, ***forrestiana***, ***globulus***, ***gunnii***, ***gummifera***, ***lansdowniana***, ***lehmannii***, ***linearis***, ***maculata***, *leuc.* var. *macrocarpa*, ***mannifera*** var. ***maculosa***, ***melliodora***, ***nicholii***, ***pauciflora***, ***polyanthemos***, ***saligna***, ***sideroxylon*** **'Rosea'**, ***spathulata***, ***torquata***, ***viminalis***
Frankenia ***pauciflora***
Goodenia ***hederacea***, ***lanata***
Goodia ***lotifolia***
Grevillea ***acanthifolia***, ***alpina***, ***aspleniifolia***, ***australis***, ***baueri***, *biternata*, ***buxifolia***, **'Canberra Gem'**, ***capitellata***, ***diminuta***, ***dimorpha***, ***endlicheriana***, **x *gaudichaudii***, ***hookerana***, ***juniperina***, ***lanigera***, ***laurifolia***, ***lavandulacea***, ***linariifolia***, ***longifolia***, ***mucronulata*** (Vic.), **'Pink Pearl'**, ***robusta***, ***rosmarinifolia***, ***rosmarinifolia*** varieties, ***sericea***, ***thelemanniana***
Hakea ***eriantha***, ***laurina***, ***multilineata***, ***petiolaris***, *purpurea*, *salicifolia*, ***sericea***, ***suaveolens***, ***teretifolia***
Hardenbergia comptoniana, *violacea*
Helichrysum ***apicalatum***, *baxteri*, 'Dargan Hill Monarch'
Hibbertia empetrifolia, *obtusifolia*, *stricta*
Homoranthus ***darwinioides***
Hypocalymma ***angustifolium***, ***cordifolium***
Indigofera australis

Isopogon ***anemonifolius, anethifolius***
Isotoma fluviatalis
Jacksonia ***scoparia***
Kennedia nigricans, rubicunda
Kunzea ambigua, capitata, parvifolia, pomifera, 'Badja Carpet'
Lambertia formosa
Leptospermum ***flavescens, juniperinum, laevigatum, lanigerum, squarrosum, scoparium*** var. ***rotundifolium***
Lechenaultia biloba, formosa
Lomatia silaifolia
Lomandra longifolia
Melaleuca armillaris , ***decussata, elliptica, ericifolia,*** *erubescens,* ***fulgens,*** *hypericifolia,* ***incana,*** *lateritia, linarifolia,* ***micromera, pulchella, steedmanni, styphelioides, thymifolia, violacea,*** *wilsonii*
Melia azedarach
Micromyrtus ***ciliata***
Mirbelia **oxylobioides**
Muehlenbeckia **axillaris**
Myoporum ***floribundum, parvifolium,*** *debile*
Olearia **phlogopappa**
Orthrosanthus multiflorus
Passiflora **cinnabarina**
Patersonia longiscapa
Philotheca salsolifolia
Phyla nodiflora
Pimelea ferruginea
Pittosporum ***phillyraeoides, revolutum, rhombifolium,*** *undulatum*
Poa **australis**
Prostanthera ***cuneata,*** *nivea,* ***rotundifolia,*** *lasianthos, ovalifolia*
Pultenaea capitellata, flexilis, ***pedunculata,*** *villosa*
Regelia ciliata
Ricinocarpus pinifolius
Scaevola ***aemula,*** *albida, humilis*
Scleranthus ***bilforus,*** *uniflorus*
Sollya ***heterophylla***
Sowerbaea ***juncea***
Stenocarpus sinuatus
Swainsona galegifolia
Tetratheca ciliata, ***ericifolia***
Tristania laurina
Thryptomene ***saxicola,*** *calycina*
Viminaria juncea
Viola hederacea
Wahlenbergia gloriosa
Westringia ***fruticosa, longifolia,*** *glabra*

For Coastal Planting

Only a minority of plants occur naturally in coastline conditions, where soils tend to be alkaline. The species below will probably require some protection from windburn, but are worth trying in this situation. Plants shown in **bold roman and *bold italics*** are suitable for extreme exposure.

Acacia baileyana, elata, glaucescens, iteaphylla, ***longifolia,*** *myrtifolia, prominens,* ***pulchella,*** *pycnantha, rotundifolia,* ***saligna, sophorae,*** *suaveolens*
Actinotus helianthi
Agonis flexuosa, juniperina
Anigozanthos flavidus
Albizia lophantha
Alyogyne huegeli
Baeckea fascicularis, ***imbricata,*** *virgata*
Banksia aspleniifolia, collina, ericifolia, ***integrifolia,*** *marginata,* ***serrata, serratifolia,*** *robur*
Callistemon citrinus, 'Harkness', *speciosus, viminalis, phoeniceus*
Calocephalus brownii
Calothamnus quadrifidus
Casuarina distyla, ***equisetifolia,*** *glauca,* ***stricta,*** *torulosa*
Cassia artemisioides
Chamelaucium uncinatum
Clematis microphylla
Correa ***alba,*** *backhousiana, pulchella,* ***reflexa***
Darwinia citriodora
Dillwynia retorta
Doryanthes excelsa
Epacris impressa, longiflora
Eucalyptus botryoides, calophylla 'Rosea', *cladocalyx nana, eximia, ficifolia, forrestiana, globulus, gummifera, lansdowniana, lehmanni, leucoxylon* 'Rosea', *maculata, perriniana, preissiana, microcorys, rubida, scoparia, torquata, viminalis, pilularis*
Frankenia pauciflora
Gompholobium grandiflorum
Grevillea banksii forsterii, brownii, capitellata, glabrata, juniperina, lanigera, lavandulacea, nudiflora, 'Pink Pearl', *rogersii, sericea, thelemanniana, tripartita, tridentifera*
Hakea bakerana, laurina, petiolaris, saligna, sericea, ***suaveolens***
Hardenbergia spp.
Helichrysum **'Diamond Head'**
Hibbertia obtusifolia, ***scandens,*** *stricta*
Hibiscus tileaceus

Hoya australis
Isopogon anemonifolius
Jacksonia scoparia
Kennedia coccinea, eximia, nigricans, prostrata, retrorsa, rubicunda
Lambertia formosa
Lagunaria patersonia
Leptospermum flavescens, juniperinum horizontalis, ***laevigatum****, rotundifolium, squarrosum*
Melaleuca ***armillaris****, decussata,* ***diosmifolia****, elliptica, ericifolia,* huegelii, ***hypericifolia****, linariifolia, micromera,* ***nesophila****, nodosa,* ***pubescens****, wilsonii*
Melia azederach
Myoporum debile, parvifolium
Pelargonium australe
Phyla nodiflora
Pimelea ***ferruginea, linifolia***
Rhagodia spinescens
Ricinocarpus pinifolius
Rulingia hermanniifolia
Scaevola calendulacea
Sollya heterophylla
Spiridium cinereum
Tetratheca ericifolia
Thomasia petiocalyx
Thryptomene saxicola 'F.C. Payne's Hybrid'
Tristania laurina
Westringia fruticosa

For Semi-Shade Positions

The following list is of plants suggested for filtered sunlight and morning sun. They will not be satisfactory in completely shaded positions.

Acacia drummondii, jibberdingensis, myrtifolia, rotundifolia
Austromyrtus tenuifolia
Baeckea crenatifolia, densifolia
Banksia spinulosa
Bauera rubioides, sessiliflora
Billardiera longiflora, scandens
Boronia spp. (except *B. megastigma*)
Brachycome spp
Callistemon spp
Calytrix spp
Clematis aristata
Correa reflexa squat, other spp
Crowea saligna, exalata
Dampiera spp
Cissus antarctica, hypoglauca
Dodonaea boroniaefolia
Eleocarpus reticulatus
Epacris spp.
Eugenia wilsonii
Grevillea aquifolium, confertifolia, dallachiana, dielsiana, intricata, lanigera, laurifolia, singuliflora, repens, rivularis, shiresii, victoriae
Guichenotia macrantha
Helichrysum spp
Hibbertia spp
Hypocalymma spp
Indigofera australis
Isopogon spp
Kunzea parvifolia
Lambertia formosa
Mazus pumilio
Melaleuca spp
Micromyrtus ciliatus
Mirbelia oxylobioides
Myoporum debile, floribundum
Olearia spp
Patersonia spp
Pimelea spp
Plectranthus parviflorus
Podocarpus lawrencei
Prostanthera spp
Pandorea spp
Pultenaea spp
Regelia ciliata
Scaevola spp
Telopea speciosissima
Tetratheca spp
Thomasia spp
Thryptomene spp
Viola hederacea
Wahlenbergia gloriosa
Westringia spp

For Moist Soils

Plants suitable for overwet (boggy) soils are shown below in ***bold italics***.

Acmena smithii
Acacia dealbata, *drummondii*, ***elata***, ***elongata***, *floribunda*, *glaucescens*, ***longissima***, *melanoxylon*, *terminalis*
Anigozanthos viridis, *flavidus*
Austromyrtus tenuifolia
Baeckea crenatifolia, *linifolia*
Bauera ***rubioides***, *sessiliflora*
Banksia ericifolia, *aspleniifolia*, *marginata*, *robur*
Backhousia citriodora
Beaufortia ***sparsa***
Billardiera longiflora
Blandfordia ***nobilis***
Boronia anemonifolia, *denticulata*, ***floribunda***, *fraseri*, *heterophylla*, ***megastigma***, *mollis*, *pilosa*, *pinnata*
Brachysema lanceolatum
Callistemon ***citrinus***, *pallidus*, *paludosus*, *phoeniceus*, *pinifolius*, *viminalis*, *violaceus*, *polandii*, *subulatus*
Callicoma serratifolia
Calytrix sullivanii, *tetragona*
Castanospermum australe
Ceratopetalum gummiferum
Casuarina ***cunninghamiana***, ***equisetifolia***, ***glauca***, *torulosa*
Cassia odorata
Correa baeuerlenni
Crowea saligna
Dampiera hederacea, *stricta*
Darwinia grandiflora
Eleocarpus reticulatus
Eugenia wilsonii
Epacris longiflora
Eucalyptus elata, *globulus*, *linearis*, *nicholii*, *saligna*, *leuhmanniana*, *spathulata*, ***robusta***, *viminalis*
Grevillea acanthifolia, *aquifolium*, *australis*, *barklyana*, *bipinnatifida*, *biternata*, *chrysophaea*, *confertifolia*, *dallachiana*, *diminuta*, *dimorpha*, *gaudichaudii*, *glabrata*, *lanigera*, *laurifolia*, *longistyla*, *miquelliana*, *oleoides*, *pinaster*, *repens*, *shiressi*, *rivularis*, *robusta*, *victoriae*
Goodenia ***humilis***
Hibbertia dentata, *obtusifolia*, ***stellaris***
Hibiscus heterophyllus
Hymenosporum flavum
Hypocalymma cordifolium
Kunzea spp.
Leptospermum spp.
Lobelia alata
Mazus ***pumilio***
Melaleuca spp. ***ericifolia***, ***squamea***
Melia azedarach
Olearia spp.
Pandorea spp.
Passiflora cinnabarina
Patersonia spp.
Pratia ***pedunculata***
Plectranthus parviflorus
Prostanthera cuneata, *lasianthos*, *mellisifolia*, *ovalifolia*, *phyllicifolia*, *rhombea*, *rotundifolia*, *stricta*, *violacea*, *walterii*
Pultenaea flexilis
Scaevola aemula
Schefflera actinophylla
Sowerbaea juncea
Stenocarpus sinuatus
Tristania conferta, ***laurina***
Viola ***hederacea***
Wahlenbergia gloriosa

For Hot, Dry Positions

Alyogyne huegelii
Albizia lophantha
Acacia baileyana, *beckleri*, *cardiophylla*, *conferta*, *cultriformis*, *decora*, *drummondii*, *floribunda*, *iteaphylla*, *podalyriifolia*, *polybotrya*, *pulchella*, *pycnantha*, *rotundifolia*, *rubida*, *saligna*, *spectabilis*, *vestita*
Brachycome multifida
Callitris spp.
Calothamnus sanguineus, *villosus*
Calytrix tetragona
Cassia spp.
Calocephalus brownii
Carpobrotus modestus
Dampiera lavundulacea, *rosmarinifolia*, *cuneata*
Dodonaea microzyga
Eremophila spp.
Eucalyptus camaldulensis, *caesia*, *cinerea*, *citriodora*, *cladocalyx nana*, *desmondensis*, *forrestiana*, *haemastoma*, *lansdowneana*, *lehmanni*, *leucoxylon* 'Rosea', *luehmanniana*, *maculata*, *mannifera*, *polyanthemos*, *scoparia*, *spathulata*, *torquata*, *viridis*
Eutaxia microphylla

Frankenia paucifolia
Goodenia lanata
Grevillea spp.
Hakea elliptica, laurina, petiolaris, purpurea, multilineata, saligna, sericea, sauveolens
Hibiscus heterophyllus
Homoranthus flavescens, darwinioides
Indigofera australis
Kennedia eximia, prorepens, prostrata
Kunzea pomifera, pulchella
Leptospermum juniperinum
Lechenaultia spp.
Melaleuca elliptica, erubescens, decussata, nesophila, wilsonii
Mirbelia dilatata
Melia azedarach
Micromyrtus ciliata
Myoporum debile, floribundum
Pelargonium rodneyanum
Pittosporum phyllyraeoides
Prostanthera baxterii, ovalifolia, aspalathoides
Phebalium squamulosum
Thryptomene baeckeacea
Sollya heterophylla
Stenocarpus sinuatus
Swainsona galegifolia
Viminaria juncea
Westringia fruticosa

For Heavy Clay Soils

Acacia decurrens, conferta, floribunda, saligna, terminalis
Banksia robur
Callistemon citrinus, 'Harkness', *paludosus, salignus, speciosus, viminalis, Violaceus*
Cassia artemisioides
Casuarina cunninghamiana, glauca, littoralis
Eucalyptus botryoides, caesia, cladocalyx, 'Nana', *globulus* spp. *bicostata, haemastoma, leucoxylon, linearis, maculata, maculosa, microcorys, mollucanna, nicholii, pauciflora, robusta, saligna, sideroxylon, rosea, tereticornis, viminalis*
Grevillea acanthifolia, alpina, brevicuspis, banksii, barklyana, confertifolia prostrate, dallachiana, 'Dargan Hill', *juniperina, lavandulacea, pinaster,* 'Pink Pearl', most Poorinda hydrids, *tridentifera*
Helichrysum bracteatum
Kunzea baxteri, parvifolia
Melaleuca armillaris, diosmifolia, erubescens, fulgens, hypericifolia, incana, lateritia, linariifolia, micromera, nesophila, pulchella, spathulata, squamea, squarrosa, styphelioides, thymifolia, wilsonii
Micromyrtus ciliata
Prostanthera walteri
Thryptomene saxicola 'Payne's hybrid'

Climbers

Billardiera spp.
Clematis spp.
Cissus antarctica
Hardenbergia comptoniana, violacea
Hibbertia dentata, scandens
Hoya australis
Kennedia coccinea, eximia, nigricans, rubicunda
Pandorea spp.
Passiflora spp.
Sollya heterophylla

For Ground Cover

Baeckea ramosissima
Bauera rubioides microphylla
Brachycome spp.
Brachysema latifolium, praemorsum
Carpobrotus modestus
Calothamnus quadrifidus prost.
Cissus antarctica
Correa decumbens
Dampiera caerulea, cuneata, diversifolia, stricta
Dodonaea procumbens
Frankenia pauciflora
Goodenia hederacea, humilis, lanata
Grevillea acanthifolia, alpina form, aquifolium var *attenuata, aquifolium Wartook, australis prost., biternata, brownii, confertifolia prost., diminuta,* x *gaudichaudii, laurifolia, obtusifolia, repens, synapheae, thelemanniana,* 'Poorinda Royal Mantle'
Hardenbergia comptoniana, violacea
Helichrysum apiculatum, 'Diamond Head'
Hemiandra pungens
Hibbertia dentata, empetrifolia, obtusifolia, procumbens, scandens, stellaris
Homoranthus flavescens
Kennedia coccinea, eximia, glabrata, microphylla, nigricans, prorepens, prostrata, rubicunda
Kunzea pomifera, 'Badja Carpet'
Leptospermum flavescens prost., juniperinum horizontalis
Mazus pumilio
Melaleuca violacea
Muehlenbeckia axillaris
Myoporum debile, parvifolium
Persoonia oxycoccoides
Pelargonium australe rodneyanum
Phyla nodiflora
Pratia pendunculata
Prostanthera denticulata
Pultenaea capitellata, cunninghamiana, pedunculata
Rhagodia nutans, spinescens
Scaevola aemula, albida
Scleranthus biflorus
Spyridium cinereum
Viola hederacea
Wahlenbergia gloriosa

Further Reading

The following books on the subject of native plants will be available from your local library.

General Texts

Australian Native Plants, Blombery (Angus & Robertson)
Australian Native Plants, Wrigley & Fagg (Collins)
Australian Native Plants for Home Gardens, Brooks (Lothian)
Birdscaping Your Garden, George Martin Adams (Rigby)
Designing Bush Gardens and *More About Bush Gardens*, Maloney & Walker (Reed)
Encyclopedia of Australian Plants (suitable for cultivation), Elliot & Jones (Lothian)
Growing Australian Plants: Shrubs, Harris (Nelson)
Growing Australian Natives in Pots, Blombery (Kangaroo)
Growing Australian Plants: Trees, Harris (Nelson)
Growing Australian Plants: Small Plants and Climbers, Harris (Nelson)
Native Gardens — how to create an Australian landscape, Molyneux & Macdonald (Nelson)
Native Trees and Shrubs of South-Eastern Australia, Leon Costermans (Rigby)
Shrubs and Trees for Australian Gardens, Lord & Willis, (Lothian)
What Wildflower is That?, Blombery (Hamlyn)
Your Australian Garden Series (David G. Stead Memorial Wildlife Foundation)

1. Propagation.
2. Mint Bushes and Their Relatives.
3. Mat and Ground Cover Plants.
4. Grevilleas
5. Callistemons and Other Bottlebrushes.
6. 200 Australian Plants For Gardens.
7. 200 Wattles for Gardens.
8. Ferns and Club Mosses.

Area Texts

A Guide to the Sydney Bushland, Fairlie (Rigby)
An Introduction to the Grampians Flora, Elliot (Algona Guides)
Australian Flora in Colour, series (Reed):
  Flowers & Plants of New South Wales & Southern Queensland:
  Flowers & Plants of Victoria:
  Flowers & Plants of Western Australia.
Collins Field Guide to the Wildflowers of S. E. Australia, Galbraith (Collins)
Field Guide to the Flowers & Plants of Victoria, Willis et al (Reed)
Flora of the Sydney Region, Beadle et al (Reed)

Specific Texts

Acacias of Australia, Simmons (Nelson)
Acacias of NSW, Armitage (SGAP)
An Introduction to the Proteaceae of Western Australia, George (Kangaroo)
Australian Climbing Plants, Jones & Gray (Reed)
Australian Ferns and Fern Allies, Jones & Clemesha (Reed)
Australian Indigenous Orchids, Dockrill (S.G.A.P.)
Eucalypts, Vols. I & II, Kelly (Nelson)
Eucalyptus Buds and Fruit, Forestry & Timber Bureau
Forest Trees of Australia, Hall et al (Aust. Gov. Printer)
Growing Ferns, Ray Best (Bay Books, Sydney)
The Banksia Book, George (Kangaroo)
Trees of New South Wales, N.S.W. Forestry Comission.

Periodicals

Australian Plants. Published as a continuing series of the Society for Growing Australian Plants, bound volumes of past issues available. (By subscription to: The Editor, SGAP, 860 Henry Lawson Drive, Picnic Point, N.S.W., 2215.)
Growing Native Plants. One issue a year by Canberra Botanic Gardens (Aust. Gov. Printer)
Parks & Wildlife. Published intermittently by National Parks & Wildlife Service of N.S.W. (By subscription to: Director, NPWLS, Box N 189, Grosvenor Street, P.O., Sydney, 2000.)

List of Common Names

There are many common names in use. These often vary from state to state. Many plants have the same common name or a number of common names. This is simply a guide.

Amulla	*Myoporum debile*
Apple Berry	*Billardiera*
Argyle Apple	*Euc. cinerea*
Australian Ivy	*Muehlenbeckia axillaris*

Bangalay	*Euc. botryoides*
Barrier Range Wattle	*Acacia beckleri*
Bird's Nest Fern	*Asplenium*
Blackbutt	*Euc. pilularis*
Blackburn	*Castanospermum australe*
Black-eyed Susan	*Tetratheca*
Black She-oak	*Casuarina littoralis*
Black Wattle	*Callicoma serratifolia, Acacia melanoxylon*
Blackwood	*Acacia melanoxylon*
Blackboy	*Xanthorrhoea australis*
Bluebell Climber	*Sollya heterophylla*
Bluebell Creeper	*Wahlenbergia*
Blueberry Ash	*Elaeocarpus reticulatus*
Bluegrass	*Poa australis*
Bloodwood	*Euc. gummifera*
Boobialla	*Myoporum*
Bottlebrush	*Callistemon, Beaufortia*
Box Leaf Wattle	*Acacia buxifolia*
Bower Plant	*Pandorea jasminoides*
Brisbane Laurel	*Pittosporum revolutum*
Broadleaf Paperbark	*Melaleuca quinquenervia*
Bronzy Boronia	*Boronia thujona*
Brown Boronia	*Boronia megastigma*
Brushbox	*Tristania conferta*
Brush myrtle	*Beaufortia*
Bush Pea	*Pultenaea*
Bushy Yate	*Euc. lehmannii*

Canberra Grass	*Scleranthus biflorus*
Candlebark	*Euc. rubida*
Cape Wattle	*Albizia lophantha*
Catspaw	*Anigozanthos humilis*
Cedar Wattle	*Acacia elata*
Chef's Cap Correa	*Correa baeuerlenii*
Christmas Bells	*Blandfordia*
Christmas Bush (NSW)	*Ceratopetalum gummiferum*
Christmas Bush (Vic)	*Prostanthera lasianthos*
Cider Gum	*Euc. gunni*
Claw Flower	*Melaleuca pulchella*
Coast Banksia	*Banksia integrifolia*
Coast Rosemary	*Westringia fruticosa*
Coast Myall	*Acacia glaucescens*
Cone Bush	*Isopogon*
Cone Flower	*Conostylis*
Coral Pea	*Kennedia*
Coral Vine	*Kennedia coccinea*
Coral Gum	*Euc. torquata*
Creeping Boobialla	*Myoporum parvifolium*
Christmas Mallee Box	*Euc. lansdowniana*
Cushion Bush	*Calocephalus brownii*
Cut-leaf Daisy	*Brachycome multifida*
Cypress Pine	*Callitris*

Dagger Hakea	*Hakea teretifolia*
Daisy	*Brachycome*
Daisy bush	*Olearia*
Darling River Pea	*Swainsona galegifolia*
Desert Cassia	*Cassia nemophila*
Drooping She-Oak	*Casuarina stricta*
Dog Rose	*Bauera rubioides*
Dogwood	*Jacksonia scoparia*
Drumsticks	*Isopogon*
Dumplings	*Billardiera scandens*
Dusky Coral Pea	*Kennedia rubicunda*
Dwarf Sugar Gum	*Euc. cladocalyx nana*

Eggs & Bacon	*Dillwynia*
Elkhorn	*Platycerium bifurcatum*
Emu Bush	*Eremophila* spp.
Eurabbie	*Euc. bicostata*
Everlastings	*Helichrysum* spp., *Helipterum* spp.

Fairy Waxflower	*Eriostemon verrucosus*
False Sarsaparilla	*Hardenbergia violacea*
Fan Flower	*Scaevola*
Fiery Bottlebrush	*Callistemon phoeniceus*
Firewheel Tree	*Stenocarpus sinuatus*
Flame Pea	*Chorizema*
Flame Tree	*Brachychiton acerifolius*
Flannel Flower	*Actinotus helianthi*
Flax Wattle	*Acacia linifolia*
Forest Oak	*Casuarina torulosa*
Forest Red Gum	*Euc. tereticornis*
Fringe Lily	*Thysanotus multiflorus*
Fringe Myrtle	*Calytrix*
Fringe Bell	*Darwinia nieldiana*
Fringed Wattle	*Acacia fimbriata*
Fuchsia Gum	*Euc. forrestiana*
Fuchsia Heath	*Epacris longiflora*

Garland Lily	*Calostemma purpurea*
Gawler Range Wattle	*Acacia iteaphylla*
Geebung	*Persoonia*
Geraldton Waxflower	*Chamaelaucium uncinatum*
Golden Grevillea	*Grevillea chrysophaea*

Golden Top	*Acacia conferta*
Golden Wattle	*Acacia pycnantha*
Golden Wreath	*Acacia saligna*
Gosford Wattle	*Acacia prominens*
Grape Grevillea	*Grevillea bipinnatifida*
Green Bottlebrush	*Callistemon pinifolius*
Green Mallee	*Euc. viridis*
Grey Spider Flower	*Grevillea buxifolia*
Grey Box	*Euc. molucanna*
Grey Gum	*Euc. punctata*
Guinea Flower	*Hibbertia*
Gungunnu, Gungurru	*Euc. caesia*
Gymea Lily	*Doryanthes excelsa*
Gum Tree	*Eucalyptus*
Gympie Messmate	*Euc. cloeziana*
Hairpin Banksia	*Banksia spinulosa*
Hairy Wattle	*Acacia vestita*
Heath	*Epacris* spp.
Heath Banksia	*Banksia ericifolia*
Hill Banksia	*Banksia collina*
Hillock Bush	*Melaleuca hypericifolia*
Honey Flower	*Lambertia formosa*
Honey Myrtle	*Melaleuca*
Honeysuckle, red	*Banksia serrata*
Honeysuckle, white	*Banksia integrifolia*
Horse-tail Casuarina	*Casuarina equisetifolia*
Hopbush	*Dodonaea*
Illawarra Flame Tree	*Brachychiton acerifolius*
Illyarie	*Euc. erythrocorys*
Ironbark, red	*Euc. sideroxylon*
Ironbark, white	*Euc. leucoxylon*
Kangaroo Thorn	*Acacia armata*
Kangaroo Paw	*Anigozanthos*
Kangaroo Vine	*Cissus antarctica*
Knife Leaf Wattle	*Acacia cultriformis*
Kurrajong	*Brachychiton populneum*
Lavendar Paperbark	*Melaleuca nesophila*
Lemon Bottlebrush	*Callistemon pallidus*
Lemon-scented Gum	*Euc. citriodora*
Lemon-scented Myrtle	*Backhousia citriodora, Darwinia citriodora*
Lemon-scented Tea-tree	*Leptospermum petersonii*
Lillypilly	*Acmena smithii*
Lilac Hibiscus	*Alyogyne huegelii*
Magenta Stork's Bill	*Pelargonium rodneyanum*
Mahogany Gum	*Euc. botryoides*
Matchheads	*Comesperma ericinum*
Matted Pea Bush	*Pultenaea pedunculata*
Mauve Boronia	*Boronia denticulata*
Melbourne Boronia	*Boronia megastigma*
Mint Bush	*Prostanthera*
Mottlecah	*Euc. maculata*
Mountain Devil	*Lambertia formosa*
Morning Flag	*Orthrosanthus multiflorus*
Mountain Grevillea	*Grevillea alpina*
Mudgee Wattle	*Acacia spectabilis*
Muntries	*Kunzea pomifera*
Narrow-leaf Peppermint	*Euc. nicholii*
Native Broom	*Viminaria juncea*
Native Cedar	*Agonis juniperina*
Native Daphne	*Pittosporum undulatum*
Native Flags	*Patersonia longiscapa*
Native Frangipanni	*Hymenosporum flavum*
Native Fuchsia	*Epacris longiflora*
Native Iris	*Dipplarena moraea, Patersonia* spp.
Nativy Ivy	*Muehlenbeckia axillaris*
Native Peach Blossom	*Hypocalymma angustifolium*
Native Rose	*Boronia serrulata*
Native Sarsaparilla	*Hardenbergia comptoniana*
Native Violet	*Viola hederacea*
Native Wistaria	*Hardenbergia comptoniana, Millettia megasperma*
Ned Kelly Grevillea	*Grevillea* 'Mason's hybrid'
Nodding Gum	*Eucalyptus nutans*
Norfolk Island Hibiscus	*Lagunaria (Fugosia) patersonia*
Old Man Banksia	*Banksia serrata*
Old Man's Beard	*Clematis*
Oven's Wattle	*Acacia pravissima*
Paperbark	*Melaleuca*
Paper Flower	*Thomasia*
Parrot Pea	*Dillwynia*
Passion Flower	*Passiflora*
Peace Myrtle	*Hypocalymma*
Pin-cushion Hakea	*Hakea laurina*
Pink Eye	*Tetratheca*
Pink Heath	*Epacris impressa*
Pink Tips	*Callistemon salignus*
Port Jackson Cypress	*Callitris rhomboidea*
Prickly Moses	*Acacia pulchella*
Prickly Paperbark	*Melaleuca styphelioides*
Purple Mallee Box	*Euc. lansdowniana*
Pyramid Tree	*Lagunaria patersonia*
Pink Buttons	*Kunzea capitata*
Queensland Nut	*Macadamia*
Queensland Silver Wattle	*Acacia podalyriifolia*
Red Bean	*Kennedia rubicunda*
Red Boronia	*Boronia heterophylla*
Red Box	*Euc. polyanthemos*
Red Cedar	*Toona australis*
Red Flowering Gum	*Euc. ficifolia*
Red Gum, Sydney	*Angophora costata*
Red Five-corners	*Styphelia tubiflora*
Red Spider Flower	*Grevillea speciosa*
Ribbon Gum	*Euc. viminalis*
Rice Flower	*Pimelea*
River Oak	*Casuarina cunninghamiana*
River Red Gum	*Euc. camaldulensis*
Robin Redbreast Bush	*Melaleuca lateritia*
Rose of the West	*Euc. macrocarpa*
Rose She-oak	*Casuarina torulosa*
Royal Grevillea	*Grevillea victoriae*
Running Postman	*Kennedia prostrata*
Rusty Apple	*Angophora costata*
Saltbush	*Rhagodia* spp.
Sand Bottlebrush	*Beaufortia squarrosa*
Sarsaparilla	*Hardenbergia*
Scarlet Runner	*Kennedia prostrata*
Scented Paperbark	*Melaleuca squarrosa*

Scribbly Gum	*Euc. haemastoma*
Sea Heath	*Frankenia pauciflora*
She-oak	*Casuarina*
Showy Bauera	*Bauera sessiliflora*
Showy Bottlebrush	*Callistemon speciosus*
Showy Wattle	*Acacia decora*
Silky Oak	*Grevillea robusta*
Silver Banksia	*Banksia marginata*
Silver Cassia	*Cassia artemisioides*
Silver Wattle	*Acacia dealbata*
Snake Bush	*Hemiandra pungens*
Snake Vine	*Hibbertia scandens*
Snow Bush	*Calocephalus brownii*
Snow-in-Summer	*Melaleuca linariifolia*
Snowy River Wattle	*Acacia boormanni*
Spear Lily	*Doryanthes*
Spider Flower	*Grevillea*
Spider Net Grevillea	*Grevillea thelemanniana*
Spinning Gum	*Euc. perinniana*
Spotted Emu Bush	*Eremophila maculata*
Spotted Gum	*Euc. maculata*
Star Bush	*Asterolasia*
Sticky Acacia	*Acacia howittii*
Sticky Boronia	*Boronia anemonifolia*
Sticky Boobialla	*Myoporum viscosum*
Stringybark Wattle	*Acacia linearifolia*
Staghorn	*Platycerium superbum*
Sugar Gum	*Euc. cladocalyx*
Swamp Banksia	*Banksia robur*
Swamp Bottlebrush	*Callistemon paludosus*
Swamp Brush Myrtle	*Beaufortia sparsa*
Swamp Mahogany	*Euc. robusta*
Swamp Mallee	*Euc. spathulata*
Swamp Oak	*Casuarina glauca*
Swamp Paperbark	*Melaleuca ericifolia*
Swamp Wattle	*Acacia elongata*
Swamp Violet	*Mazus pumilio*
Swan River Pea	*Brachysema lanceolata*
Sweet Apple Berry	*Billardiera cymosa*
Sydney Blue Gum	*Euc. saligna*
Sydney Golden Wattle	*Acacia longifolia*
Sydney Peppermint	*Euc. piperita*
Sydney Red Gum	*Angophora costata*

Tallowwood	*Euc. microcorys*
Tasmanian Blue Gum	*Euc. globulus*
Tea-tree	*Leptospermum*
Tick Bush	*Kunzea*
Tinsel Lily	*Calectasia cyanea*
Tree Waratah	*Oreocallis*
Turpentine	*Syncarpia glomulifera*
Tufted Darwinia	*Darwinia fascicularis*
Umbrella Tree	*Schefflera actinophylla*
Varnish Grevillea	*Grevillea dielsiana*
Velvet Bush	*Lasiopetalum dasyphyllum*
Violet	*Viola* or *Mazus*
Wallangarra Wattle	*Acacia adunca*
Wallum Banksia	*Banksia serratifolia*
Waratah	*Telopea speciosissima*
Water Gum	*Tristania laurina*
Wattle	*Acacia*
Waxflower	*Eriostemon*
Wax Plant	*Hoya australis*
Wedding Bush	*Ricinocarpus pinifolius*
Wedge Pea	*Gompholobium*
Weeping Baeckea	*Baeckea linifolia*
Weeping Boree	*Acacia vestita*
Weeping Bottlebrush	*Callistemon viminalis*
Weeping Myrtle	*Agonis flexuosa*
Western Silver Wattle	*Acacia polybotrya*
White Cedar	*Melia azedarach*
White Peppermint	*Euc. linearis*
White Sally	*Acacia floribunda*
Wild Parsley	*Lomatia silaifolia*
Willow Bottlebrush	*Callistemon salignus*
Willow Gum	*Euc. scoparia*
Willow Myrtle	*Agonis flexuosa*
Willow Peppermint	*Euc. elata*
Wonga Vine	*Pandorea pandorana*
Yellow Bloodwood	*Euc. eximia*
Yellow Box	*Euc. melliodora*
Yellow Mountain Bell	*Darwinia collina*
Yellow Top Ash	*Euc. luehmanniana*

Mallee

Eucalyptus caesia
" pauciflora (snow gum)

Anigozanthos - Kangaroo paws

Banksia bauri - Wooly banksia
" ? - popcorn smell

Grevillea - Robyn Gordon
lanigera
aquifolium

Leucospermum
Erica
Protea

Leucadendron argenteum

Leptospermum - manuka, tea tree
Agathis - Kauri
Phormium - flax

Astelia - silver sword
inner

Tetra